101 AMAZING CARD TRICKS

♣ ♦ ♥ ♠

BOB LONGE

Sterling Publishing Co., Inc. New York

Library of Congress Cataloging-in-Publication Data

Longe, Bob, 1928–
    101 amazing card tricks / by Bob Longe.
      p.   cm.
    Includes index.
    ISBN 0-8069-0342-2
    1. Card tricks. I. Title. II. Title: One hundred one amazing
card tricks. III. Title: One hundred and one amazing card tricks.
    GV1549.L52   1993
    795.4'38—dc20   93-23861
                                                        CIP

40 39 38 37 36 35

Published in 1993 by Sterling Publishing Co., Inc.
387 Park Avenue South, New York, NY 10016
© 1993 by Bob Longe
Distributed in Canada by Sterling Publishing
℅ Canadian Manda Group, 165 Dufferin Street,
Toronto, Ontario, Canada M6K 3H6
Distributed in the United Kingdom by GMC Distribution Services,
Castle Place, 166 High Street, Lewes, East Sussex, England BN7 1XU
Distributed in Australia by Capricorn Link (Australia) Pty. Ltd.
P.O. Box 704, Windsor, NSW 2756, Australia

Sterling ISBN-13: 978-0-8069-0342-2
    ISBN-10: 0-8069-0342-2

For information about custom editions, special sales, premium and
corporate purchases, please contact Sterling Special Sales
Department at 800-805-5489 or specialsales@sterlingpub.com.

CONTENTS

CONTENTS 5

INTRODUCTION

In this book you'll find tricks ranging from the marvelous to the hilarious. Some, of my own invention, appear in print for the first time. I have eliminated sleights from many fine effects. In fact, about three-quarters of *all* the tricks require no sleight of hand whatever.

Here you will find card tricks that are unique, engaging, mystifying, challenging, and—most important—entertaining, and they're all well within your grasp.

NOW YOU SEE IT— NOW YOU DON'T

Some of the better tricks in this book require some sleight of hand. Here you'll find the sleights you'll need.

♦ The Hindu Shuffle ♦

I'm convinced that the *Hindu Shuffle* is the most important sleight for you to learn. If you want to get into advanced card trickery, you have to be able to do several things: force a card, control a card, and false shuffle so that a group of cards will remain in order and be accessible to you. All of these can be accomplished with the *Hindu Shuffle*. (*The Hindu Shuffle Force* appears on page 33).

♦ The Shuffle ♦

Hold the deck in your right hand, with your left held in front, palm up (Illus. 1). The cards are brought to the left hand, where the second and third fingers on the right side and the thumb on the left side grasp a small packet from the top. The right

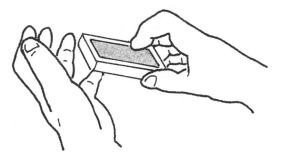

Illus. 1. Hold the deck in your right hand, with your left held in front, palm up.

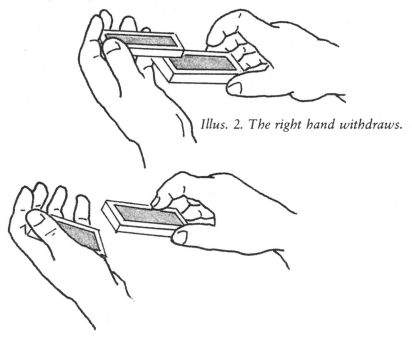

Illus. 2. The right hand withdraws.

Illus. 3. The small packet drops into your left hand.

hand withdraws (Illus. 2). The small packet drops into the left hand (Illus. 3).

Repeat this until you have only a small packet in the right hand; this is dropped on top.

◆ False Hindu Shuffle ◆

You wish to retain one card or several cards on top of the deck. As with the regular *Hindu Shuffle*, draw off a pile and drop it into your left hand. When your right hand returns to have another packet drawn off, the right second and third fingers and thumb pick up a portion of the packet just dropped (Illus. 4). As you study the illustration, you will note that a natural break is held between the packet you have picked up and the rest of the cards in the right hand.

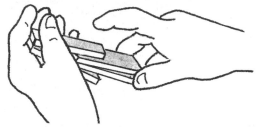

Illus. 4. The right second and third fingers and thumb pick up a portion of the packet just dropped.

Continue drawing off packets as in the normal *Hindu Shuffle*. The second last packet will be all the cards above the break you're holding. The last packet, consisting of the cards originally on top of the deck, is dropped on top.

At first, you will probably hesitate slightly as you sneak the small packet. Practise, trying to make the move as smooth as possible.

◆ Controlling a Card with the Hindu Shuffle ◆

Fan the cards from hand to hand for the free selection of a card. As the card is shown around, square up the deck.

Draw off three or four packets in a *Hindu Shuffle*, and then stop and hold out the cards in the left hand for the return of the chosen card on top of the pile. After the card is returned, continue the *Hindu Shuffle*, but when you draw off the first packet, pick up several cards with the right hand, as with the false shuffle. Naturally, this pile is dropped on the deck last, bringing the chosen card to the top.

◆ Table False Cut ◆

Here's a false cut requiring no sleight of hand. You must, however, practise it until you can do it smoothly.

Mentally divide the deck into thirds. The top third is 1, the second third is 2, and the bottom third is 3. So, as the deck sits on the table, it is:

1

2

3

With the right hand, cut off the top two-thirds and move this bunch four or five inches to the right of the original pile. Leave the bottom half there, and drop the rest in the middle. The situation now is this:

3   1   2

Don't pause. Pick up pile 2 and drop it on pile 3. Pick up pile 1, and drop it on all.

Try this one. If done smoothly, without pause, it is quite deceptive.

◆ The Triple-Cut Control ◆

This is, in effect, a cut of the deck, bringing the chosen card to the top or bottom.

You've fanned the cards and you've had a spectator choose one. After he has looked at it, you spread the cards once more for the insertion of the card. As you close up the fan, lift the portion above his card slightly with your right fingertips and hold about a quarter-inch break with your left little finger (Illus. 5). The left hand holds the cards in the dealing position, but the right hand takes control of the deck (Illus. 6). The

Illus. 5. Hold about a quarter-inch break with your left little finger.

Illus. 6. The left hand holds the cards in the dealing position, but the right hand takes control of the deck.

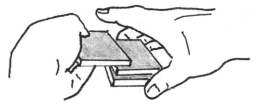

Illus. 7. Take a small packet from the bottom of the deck and place it on top.

right hand naturally holds the two halves separate with the right thumb, and the left little finger is withdrawn.

With the left hand, take a small packet from the bottom of the deck and place it on top, lifting the right first finger (or the right first and second fingers) to allow it to pass (Illus. 7). The left hand now takes about half of the cards below the break and places this group on top. Finally, the left hand takes the rest of the cards below the break and places them on top.

Originally, this was a double-cut; the additional cut makes it somewhat more deceptive.

To bring a card to the bottom, simply take the little-finger break below the chosen card.

◆ The Glide ◆

This sleight is easy to do and is essential to the performance of many excellent tricks. You show the bottom card and apparently place it on the table; in fact, you deal down the second card from the bottom.

Hold the deck face down from above with the left hand, fingers on the left side and thumb on the right (Illus. 8). Tilt

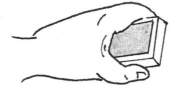

Illus. 8. Hold the deck face down from above with the left hand.

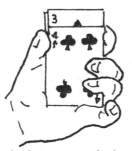

Illus. 9. Draw back the bottom card about half an inch with the second and third fingers of the left hand.

back the hand to show the bottom card, and then turn the cards face down again. As you reach under with the tips of the right second and third fingers to take the card, it is drawn back about half an inch with the second and third fingers of the left hand (Illus. 9). The right fingers draw out the second card from the bottom, and the right thumb grips it on top as it slides out. The card is placed face down on the table.

The left little finger pushes the bottom card even with the deck.

MENTAL MAGIC

These tricks should be dressed up with occult or psychic jargon. With occult patter, toss in words and expressions like, "ancient rites," "spirits," "mystic," etc.

With psychic patter, you are usually trying to enhance the "mental waves." "You must deal the same number as the card you chose to strengthen the telepathic vibrations," or, "Some numbers are harder to receive than others, so would you please deal . . . " Here you use words and expressions like, "psychic phenomena," "telepathy," "precognition," "extrasensory perception," "mind reading," "mentalism," "thought waves," etc.

♦ Mystic Nine ♦

Hand the deck to a volunteer and turn away. "Please shuffle the cards thoroughly. Now, in any way you wish, select a spot card and place it face up on the table. This is your card. Please remember the name. Now concentrate on the suit and value."

Pretend to cogitate. "I'm not getting it. Would you quietly deal next to the card a number of cards equal to its value." Briefly pause. "No, that doesn't work. Would you deal that same number on the *other* side of your selected card." Again pause briefly. "Mind reading doesn't seem to be working. I'll try for something mystic. As you know, the mystic number is nine. Please turn your selected card face down and deal on top of it nine cards."

When he has finished dealing, say, "That doesn't help. Set the deck aside. Gather up the three piles and give them a thorough shuffle."

Turn back and take the packet. Fan through, apparently studying the cards. Actually, you count them. Do this unobtrusively by counting in groups of three. Subtract ten from the total and divide by two. This gives you the value of the chosen card. For example, if you count 26 cards, you subtract 10, giving you 16. Divide 16 by 2, giving you 8. The chosen card is an eight.

Let us assume the spectator chose an eight. Continue studying the cards. If there is only one eight, remove it, ask the spectator to name his card, and show your selection.

If there are two eights, slip one to the top and one to the bottom. Set the pile down. Ask for the name of the card. Either show the top card or turn the deck over, showing the bottom card.

If there are four eights, ask if the color is black. Whatever the answer, you are down to two cards and can finish as above.

If there are three eights, again ask if the color is black, eliminating one color. You will be left with either two cards or one.

♦   My Time Is Your Time   ♦

Remove from the deck the cards of one suit, except for the king. Place these twelve cards face up in the form of a clock, the ace at one o'clock, the two at two o'clock, etc. The jack goes at 11 o'clock, and the queen goes at 12 o'clock. Place the remainder of the deck into two fairly equal piles on the table. Ask a volunteer to think of one of the cards. Pick up one of the two piles and place the cards of the clock on top one at a time, starting with the ace and ending with the queen.

Hand the spectator the other pile. Set your pile on the table. Say, "Think about the number you selected. While I turn away, deal that number from your pile onto the pile on the table."

When you turn back, pick up the pile on the table. Take the cards from the spectator and place them *on the bottom* of your pile. At this point, you may decide to perform a false cut, but this isn't essential.

Hand the deck to your volunteer and ask him to deal the cards one at a time on the table. He may drop each card wherever he wishes. Pass your hand over the dealt cards as he goes along, feeling the vibrations. Note where he drops the thirteenth card. Let him go a few more, and then drop your hand on the thirteenth. "This is it," you declare. "It feels right." He names his card. Sure enough.

◆ It *Is* Magic ◆

In this trick, the spectator keeps the cards throughout. Hand the deck to a spectator and turn your back. "Please shuffle the cards," you say. "Now think of a number from one to ten, and then deal two piles with that number in each pile. Deal very quietly."

When your volunteer is finished, say, "Choose either pile, and look at the bottom card of that pile. Please let everyone see the card. Now place that pile, with your card on the bottom, on top of the deck. Set the other pile aside for now."

"Let's see if the signs are right. Take a look at the top card of the deck. Is it black or red?"

Whatever the answer, continue: "Place that card face down on the table. What color is the next card?" After the answer, say, "Place that card face down on top of the first card you put on the table. Very slowly, please continue giving me the color of the cards and placing the cards face down on the pile."

While your helper does so, murmur things like, "Excellent. Superb. This looks very promising."

Actually, you are counting the cards he is dealing out. After he has dealt eleven cards, stop him, saying, "That's fine. You can stop." (I keep track of the number of cards in the traditional manner—with my fingers.)

Tell the spectator to pick up the pile he just dealt and place it on top of the deck. Then say, "Set the deck aside for a moment. Now pick up your other small pile and tell me how many face cards there are."

Whatever he tells you, express gratification. "Now put that pile on top of the deck."

His chosen card is now twelfth from the top. Face the group. Ask your assistant to name his card, and then have him spell out, "Here is my card," taking off one card for each letter in the spelling and turning the last card face up. Work him through it slowly, but by no means take the cards yourself.

♦ Magic Spell ♦

Fan through the deck, saying, "I'm going to select a card that you *will* think of, and several more that you cannot possibly think of."

First set the three of diamonds face down on the table. On top of that, place the eight of diamonds. Next the jack of diamonds. The next three cards may be either hearts or spades: seven, five, two. The last is the ace of clubs. Illus. 10 shows the proper order as you look at the cards.

You might try this mnemonic: *Thirty-eight jacks saved (seven) fifty-two aces.* 3, 8, J, 7, 5, 2, A. The first three are diamonds; the next three may be either spades or hearts. The last is the ace of clubs.

"Seven cards . . . my lucky number," you comment. Give the cards several rapid overhand cuts, as though shuffling. The basic order remains the same. Hand the cards to a spectator, asking him to fan them in front of him, looking at the faces.

Illus. 10. This shows the proper order as you look at the cards.

He is to think of one of the cards. You avert your head. Then he cuts the cards—more than once, if he chooses.

You take back the group and study the faces. Nod knowingly and cut the *eight* to the top of the pile. Hand him the pile and ask him to name his card. He is then to spell out the name, transferring one card from top to bottom for each letter in the spelling. Have him turn over the last card of the spelling; it is the card he thought of.

"I *knew* you'd take that," you declare.

There is an exception in the spelling. If the spectator spells out the three of diamonds, he must not turn over the last card of the spelling, but the *next* one.

The trick is based on the idea that you have selected cards that spell out with a different number of letters. Only the first two diamonds have the same number of letters in their spelling.

♦ A Simple Swindle ♦

This quick mental trick is a total swindle. Despite its simplicity, it never fails to fool.

Ask a spectator to shuffle the deck. If, as he does so, you're fortunate enough to catch a glimpse of the bottom card, take the deck back immediately. If not, you might learn the name of the bottom card using one of the methods given in *The Hindu Shuffle Force*, page 33. In any instance, you must know the bottom card.

Ask the spectator to give you a number from ten to twenty. Deliberately count the cards into a pile on the table. When you come to the card at the spectator's number, deal it face down near the spectator and ask him to turn it over. As he does so, transfer the remaining cards from your left hand to your right, taking them palm down. Casually set them on top of the pile you dealt on the table. *Leave the cards there.*

Suppose the spectator gives you the number 13. Deal off 12 cards and deal the 13th in front of the spectator. Drop the remaining cards on top of the pile on the table as he turns the card over. It is, say, the queen of clubs. "So," you say, "the queen of clubs is the 13th card from the top. Easy enough. We just look at it. But what do you suppose is the 13th card from the bottom?"

With great effort, you arrive at the name of the card you peeked at on the bottom of the deck. Suppose it was the nine of hearts. You might say, "Queen of clubs is a black card. So the other is probably red. A heart, I would say." Concentrate. "It can't be a face card, but it's probably fairly high. An odd card, I think. A nine. Yes. The nine of hearts."

Have the spectator pick up the deck, turn it face up, and count off 13 cards. The 13th is the one you foretold.

◆ Significant Pointers ◆

In card magic, certain cards are referred to as "pointers" or "pointer cards." They are so called because most of the pips on each card point in one direction. Twenty-two of the 52 cards in the deck are pointers. In clubs, hearts, and spades,

these are the pointers: A, 3, 5, 6, 7, 8, 9. These cards point
when the majority of spots are right-side up. The only diamond
pointer is the seven, when its center pip is in the top portion
of the card.

When the faces of these cards are arranged right-side up
and one is turned end for end, it can be easily identified. The
idea is quite old, but is hardly known at all to the general
public.

In most effects using pointers, the cards are set up in advance.
My version eliminates the prearrangement, and attempts to
turn a weakness into a strength.

The deck you use, preferably a borrowed one, shouldn't
have a one-way design on the back. The reason is simple: When
you have the pointers set up properly, the backs will also be
set up; as your assistant works with the face-down cards, he
may well notice this.

Start by shuffling the cards, setting them down, and asking
a spectator to cut off about half the deck. You take the other
half. "I am going to try to read your mind," you say. "This
may not work unless, between us, we choose cards we can
both be happy with. So I would like you to go through your
stack, take out about ten cards that you feel good about, and
toss them face up on the table. And I'll do the same with my
cards. By the way, please don't take out face cards. They're
much too obvious." And also they're not pointers.

As the spectator tosses his choices face up in front of him,
you place yours in front of you, overlapping so that the faces
can be seen. You select ten pointers, or as many as you can.
Fan the cards faces towards you and, as you remove each card,
place it down so that it is pointed properly. When you choose
a card that isn't pointed correctly, take it at the top and revolve
it as you place it on the table.

The rest of the cards are set aside. Say, "Now we'll make
sure we have cards agreeable to both of us. You select a card
from my group, and then I'll take one from yours."

You should end up with ten cards (or as many as possible)

face up in your left hand, with all ten pointed properly. Take
his first selection and place it in your left hand. Select a pointer
from his cards and place it on top of the first card. If it isn't
pointed correctly, take it at the far end when you pick it up.
Turn your hand so that fingers and thumb are at the bottom
as you bring the card in front of your face to study it. Finally
nod your head and add the card to the ones in your left hand.
This effectively turns the card around.

If the spectator has only a few pointers, take those at your
turn and then tell him you are tired of choosing, that he should
choose several from your selections.

Turn the cards in your hand face down and hand them to
the spectator, asking him to shuffle. Pantomime an overhand
shuffle, indicating this is the type he should perform. Gather
up all the remaining cards into one face-down pack. "In a
moment, I will turn away," you say, "and here is what I'd like
you to do." Cut off about ten cards from the pack and demonstrate as you speak. "Fan the cards in front of you and merely
think of a particular card. Take that card and place it face
down in front of you." Demonstrate. "Shuffle the rest as you
concentrate on your card." Do a few overhand shuffles. "Place
the rest of the cards on top of your card and tap the pack
three times. It sounds silly, but it's very important." Show him
how. "Then pick up the pile and shuffle it some more." Demonstrate.

Follow the above instructions with a packet of pointers and
you will see what happens: The chosen card is turned the other
way among the pointers.

You may want to repeat the demonstration to make sure
the spectator understands. Turn away while the spectator per-
forms his task. When he's done, turn back and take the packet.
Fan through the cards, find the reversed pointer, and remove
it, saying, "This one somehow seems to vibrate." Take it at
the top and place it on the table, revolving it as you do so.
When you add it to the other pointers, it will be turned the
right way, and you are ready for a repeat.

♦ Impossible Prediction ♦

You correctly predict the number of face-up cards that will be in the deck, something over which, ostensibly, you have no control.

"Let's try an experiment in precognition. I'll make a prediction, using two cards."

Remove two cards from the deck and place them face down on the table, saying that your prediction is the total of these two. The prediction should total somewhere from 15 to 20. A nine and a seven, for example, could be removed—the prediction being 16.

Hand the deck to a volunteer, turn away, and say, "Please make two piles of cards, say a dozen or so in each pile. You don't need to have the same number in each pile." Pause. "Pick up one of the piles and turn some cards face up. You can turn over a group of cards or cards at different places in the pile." Pause. "Now turn the same number face up wherever you wish in the other pile."

When he is done, tell him to place one of the piles on top of the deck and to hide the other pile. Put your hands behind your back and ask the spectator to give you the deck.

With the cards behind your back, face the spectators and say, quite truthfully, "Let's see if I can make my prediction come true." Babble on as you count off the number of cards in your prediction and turn them face up on top. The best way is to count them one under the other.

Bring the cards forward and tell the spectator to place his other pile on top. "The question is," you say, "how many face-up cards do we now have?"

Fan through the deck, tossing out and counting the face-up cards as you come to them. When your helper turns over your two prediction cards, he finds that the total precisely matches the number of face-up cards.

♦ Pocket Pool ♦

For this one you require only a deck of cards and a natural instinct to cheat and deceive.

Beforehand, place these cards in a convenient pocket: ace of clubs, two of hearts, four of spades, and eight of diamonds. The best bet is to place the cards in the right pants pocket so that they face inward, the ace of clubs on top. It's easy to remember ace, two, four, eight. And the suits can be remembered by using the mnemonic CHaSeD—for clubs, hearts, spades, diamonds.

Have the rest of the deck shuffled. Place the deck in the same pocket as your four stacked cards, making sure that your stack is on top of the deck, readily accessible.

Ask the spectators to agree on one card among themselves. Ask for the name of the card. When told, say, "I'm going to attempt something really unusual. First, I am going to try to match the suit of the card."

As you speak, stick your hand into your pocket and thumb through the top four cards to the one of the appropriate suit. Remove this card from the pocket, holding it face down. "What was the name of that suit?"

Turn the card over, showing you have matched the suit.

Illus. 11. The four cards shown here can match the value of any card in the deck.

"I am going to try to match the value of the card you thought of."

Now you will remove additional cards to match the value. With the four cards (including the one representing the suit), you can match any value in the deck.

An example: The chosen card is the queen of hearts. You first bring out the two of hearts, matching the suit. When told the choice is the queen, say, "The queen, as you know, has a value of 12. So I must find cards to total 12." Remove the four from your pocket. "A four." Remove the eight. "An eight. Eight and four is 12. I have matched your chosen card." Study the four cards in Illus. 11, and you will see how you can match the value of any card in the deck.

You have many opportunities to perform a real miracle. You have four chances to match the chosen card exactly. And an additional 12 chances to produce a card of the proper suit and another of the proper value. This means that about 31% of the time you will absolutely astonish.

♦ The Perfect Match ♦

Working on a trick in which a spectator—apparently randomly—matches kings and queens by suit, I decided to try the same principle on a grander scale. After smoothing out the bumps, I had one of my most startling effects.

The effect is this: You place a card face down on the table. A spectator tries to match it in value. This is done several times. It turns out that the spectator has matched each card perfectly.

The trick, a variation of the "one ahead" system, is actually quite simple. If you follow with a deck of cards, you'll catch on immediately.

Have a volunteer cut off half the deck. You take the other half. "Please take out 13 cards," you say, "one of each kind—

ace, two, three, and so on, right up to the king. The suits don't matter. I'll do the same."

Your cards must be arranged in order, starting with the ace on top, two second, and the bottom card the king. You may do this by fanning the cards towards you, drawing out the ace with the right hand, and then drawing out the two in front of the ace. Continue until all are in order. You may also pile them face down on the table, placing the king down first and working upward. Possibly you may be missing a value from your half deck; simply get one from the spectator. And he may have to get a card or two from you. When I have to ask for more than one card, I will say, "Do you have a five? I get the feeling I'm playing a game of *Fish*." When you're finished, straighten your pile and casually give the cards a long series of overhand cuts, as though you were shuffling.

Meanwhile, you patter. As with most tricks, don't tell the spectators exactly what you expect to accomplish. As you gather your cards, you might come up with a charming mystical origin for the trick.

By this time, you should have given the cards a number of rapid overhand cuts, which, of course, won't change the basic order. Tip the cards so that you can see the bottom card. Deal the cards into a face-down row on the table. This is the order as you look at them:

8 9 10 J Q K A 2 3 4 5 6 7

How do you accomplish this? Suppose you peeked at the three on the bottom of the deck. You know that the top card must be the four. So you deal it several inches from the right edge of the table. Deal the five to the right of it; then the six and the seven. You have run out of table. Look a bit perplexed. Then go to the far left and deal the other cards from left to right, ending up with the three. The illusion is created that the cards are in no particular order.

Casually push your ace forward and move it to the right end of the row, above your cards:

$$\text{A}$$
$$8 \quad 9 \quad 10 \quad \text{J} \quad \text{Q} \quad \text{K} \qquad 2 \quad 3 \quad 4 \quad 5 \quad 6 \quad 7$$

Tell your helper to look over his cards and pick one out, but not to make it too obvious. This is to prevent him from picking an ace, which would make for a very short trick. He is to place his selected card face up on top of the one you shoved out. If he *should* choose an ace, tell him, joshingly, "No, no, that's far too obvious. Pick something else."

Suppose he places a jack on top of your ace. You now place your jack next to your face-down ace, requesting that he place another card face up on top of it. In parentheses is the spectator's face-up card.

$$\qquad\qquad\qquad\qquad\qquad\qquad\qquad \text{J} \quad \text{(J)A}$$
$$8 \quad 9 \quad 10 \qquad \text{Q} \quad \text{K} \qquad 2 \quad 3 \quad 4 \quad 5 \quad 6 \quad 7$$

Again, make sure he doesn't choose the ace. You'd like to get at least four pairs down before the ace is chosen.

Assume that the spectator places a four on top of the jack. Casually push out your four, placing it next to your face-down jack, and say, "Okay, put a card face up on this one."

$$\qquad\qquad\qquad\qquad\qquad\qquad\qquad 4 \quad \text{(4)J} \quad \text{(J)A}$$
$$8 \quad 9 \quad 10 \qquad \text{Q} \quad \text{K} \qquad 2 \quad 3 \qquad 5 \quad 6 \quad 7$$

Next he chooses his nine. You push out your nine, placing it next to the others, and repeat your request.

$$\qquad\qquad\qquad\qquad\qquad\qquad 9 \quad \text{(9)4} \qquad \text{(4)J} \quad \text{(J)A}$$
$$8 \qquad 10 \qquad \text{Q} \quad \text{K} \qquad 2 \quad 3 \qquad 5 \quad 6 \quad 7$$

This time he chooses, say, the two. Place your two next to the others and urge another choice.

$$\qquad\qquad\qquad\qquad\qquad 2 \quad \text{(2)9} \quad \text{(9)4} \quad \text{(4)J} \qquad \text{(J)A}$$
$$8 \qquad 10 \qquad \text{Q} \quad \text{K} \qquad 3 \qquad 5 \quad 6 \quad 7$$

At this point, it doesn't matter if he chooses the ace. Continue on until he does select the ace. Sometimes all the cards are used: sometimes only five pairs. Assume that your helper now places the ace on top of your two. Say, "Let's not overdo it. This should be enough to give us an idea." Take the remaining cards from the spectator and set them aside. Also, gather up the rest of your face-down cards and set them aside.

On the table, you have this:

(A)2   (2)9   (9)4   (4)J   (J)A

Gather up the cards from the right. With your right hand, pick up the pair on the far right (or draw it towards you) and place it into your left hand. Take the pair that is now on the right and place it on top of the other in the left hand. Continue until all the cards are in a single pile.

"The magic number is three, so we must have the cards cut at least three times." Have three spectators give the cards a complete cut. You must end up with a face-down card on top. If that isn't the case, cut a face-down card to the top, saying, "Even I'll give them a cut."

Now deal the cards out in pairs. Deal the top card onto the table and deal the next (face-up) card on top of it. Deal the third card a little distance away, and the fourth card on top of it. Continue until you have dealt out all the pairs. "I have my doubts about this, but we might as well see it through."

Invite the spectator to pick out a pair. Turn over the bottom card, showing that you have a match. "Good! A match."

Continue showing the matches one by one. When you show the final match, say, "I can't believe it. One hundred percent! Congratulations!"

Notes:

1. One key to the trick is that you don't hesitate unduly in making your face-down choices. At first it may seem difficult to pick out a face-down card matching the spectator's previous choice, particularly if you get up to seven or more pairs. If in trouble, chatter for a moment as you check out the other *face-up* cards. This will enable you to fill in the gaps on the table and see which card is the proper one. With practice, you will find the selection becomes fairly easy.

2. Occasionally you will make an error, leading to a mismatch of two or more pairs. Don't panic; accept it. The spectator still did very well.

♦ E.S.P. ♦

Here we have an unusual trick in which the glide—performed repeatedly—seems perfectly natural and is never suspected. It is an adaptation of a trick which requires special cards with symbols on their faces. In my version, an ordinary deck of cards is used.

Because the effect is roughly similar to that of *The Perfect Match*, it works especially well as a follow-up.

Fan through the deck, faces towards you, pushing up all the cards from nine to ace. Each should be raised about 1½". Grasp the cards you pushed up with one hand and the lower cards with your other hand. Strip out the cards from nine to ace, and set the others aside. As you do all this, explain, "I think this group has exceptional extrasensory perception. We'll test it."

By this time, you should have the cards stripped from the deck. Hand the rest of the cards to a spectator, saying, "I need all the face cards, nines, and aces. Would you see if I left any in here, and I'll check these out."

Fan your cards, faces towards you, and remove any nine, placing it face down on the table. Place a ten face down on top of it, and then a jack, a queen, a king, and an ace. The suits don't matter. Starting with a nine, place another sequence on the pile. Do this two more times. You should be out of cards, and the pile should have, from top to bottom, four sequences of 9, 10, J, Q, K, A. Clearly, you should perform this setup as rapidly as possible.

Thanking the spectator, take the remainder of the cards from him and place them aside. Even up your stacked cards, saying, "I guess they're all here. Now we must have them cut three times. As you know, three is a magic number."

Have three spectators give the cards a complete cut. Single cuts, of course, do not change the basic order.

"As you know, the pyramid has most unusual powers, so I am going to deal some cards in a pyramid."

Deal the top ten cards face down in this order:

From the spectators' point of view, you have formed a rough pyramid with the cards.

"Now we're going to test your E.S.P." Holding the deck in the glide grip, draw off the *bottom* card. "I am going to ask a number of you if you think the card in my hand matches in value a particular one on the table." (Later, the card will not actually be in your hand, but on the bottom of the deck.) "If you say it matches, I'll put it on the card like this." Still gripping the card, place it crosswise on card number 10. Pick it up. "If you say it *doesn't* match, I'll put it on like this." Still retaining your grip, place the card directly on card number 10, so that it covers the card completely.

Place the card in your hand on top of the deck. *This is critical!* The bottom card must be placed on top for the trick to work.

With your right hand, point to card number 10, the last card you dealt down. Tap the underside of the bottom card, saying to a spectator, "Do you think this card will match the one on the table or not?" Suppose he says that it *will* match. Perform the glide and place the card face down and crosswise on card number 10. "So the card goes on crosswise," you explain.

You proceed to work in the exact reverse to the order in which you placed the cards on the table; you will start at 10 and end at 1. As you go along, choose different persons to indicate whether the card matches or not. If a person says it matches, perform the glide and place the card crosswise on the appropriate card on the table. If a person says it doesn't match, simply take the bottom card and place it so that it covers the card in question. Each time, ask the person, "Match or no match?"

After doing card number 1—the last of those on the table—set the remaining cards onto the pile you had initially set aside.

"Let's check the rejects first. Many of the nonmatches should work out." Take up a pair of nonmatches from anywhere on the table, show that the cards don't match, and set the pair face down on top of the discards. Do the same for all the other nonmatches.

"Now if I'm right, and you ladies and gentlemen are loaded with E.S.P., some of these others should match up." Pick up a pair of crossed cards. Very deliberately turn them over, one with each hand. Show that they match and set them down together face up.

Turn over the others the same way, each time expressing approval of the audience's psychic ability. After showing the last matching pair, look over the results with great satisfaction. Applaud the group, saying, "You're fantastic." I like to conclude by saying with a twinkle, "I've tried this for years, and this is the first time it ever came out perfectly."

Make sure you have no more than four *consecutive* matches. If you have four, and a spectator says that he thinks the fifth pair will match as well, say, "No, it's my turn, and I say they won't match." Deal the bottom card down to make a non-matching pair. Continue to the end normally.

Notes:

1. When making the setup, some persons can fan the cards in front of them and sort them without setting them down. They hold the fanned cards in the left hand and start by drawing out an ace with the right hand. Then they draw out a king so that it's in front of the ace. They continue through all the rest of the cards. If you can do this, the setup goes much faster. But don't worry if you have trouble with it; the other method works out fine.

2. When I ask a person whether we have a match, I already have drawn back the bottom card ½″ or so in the glide move. Then, depending on the answer, I instantly take either the second card from the bottom, or reach back a bit and take the bottom card. The drawing out of the card is virtually simultaneous with the answer. Trickery is never suspected.

◆   **Count On It**   ◆

Have the deck shuffled. Take the deck back and prepare to fan through the cards, faces towards you. Note the bottom card. You're going to arrange for that card to become the 21st from the top. At the same time, you're going to find a card of the same color and value as that card, take it out of the deck, and place it face down as your prediction card.

Suppose the bottom card is the ten of diamonds. You will be hunting for the ten of hearts. Say, "I'll have to find a prediction card," as you begin fanning through the cards and counting them. When you have fanned out nine or ten, pause, shake your head, and place the group on top. Continue fanning and counting, picking up at the next number. When you reach 21, shake your head, and place that group on top. The 21st card from the top is now the ten of diamonds.

Continue fanning to the ten of hearts, take it from the deck, and place it face down on the table. Suppose, however, that the ten of hearts turns up in that first 21 cards. Pull it from the deck, studying it carefully. No, it won't do. Place it well above the middle of the deck. Continue your count from the point where you pulled the ten of hearts. After you arrange for the ten of diamonds to be 21st from the top, continue fanning to the ten of hearts. This time, take it from the deck and place it face down on the table.

Get a volunteer and say to him, "You are about to select a card. If I have correctly foretold the future, it should match my prediction in color and value."

Have the volunteer cut off a small packet of cards. He must take fewer than 21 cards. You now deal off 20 cards face up from right to left, overlapping so that the values can be seen.

"You don't know how many cards you have cut off, right?" Of course not. "It could be *any* number. Please count them." Turn your head aside while he does so.

When he's finished, tell him to start at his right and count that many over in the row on the table. He is to pull out the card he lands on.

Turn over your prediction card. Right again!

◆ Secret Signals ◆

For this stunt you need a partner. Don't be put off. You and a friend can have great fun with this, and you can provide a puzzling and entertaining demonstration of mind reading. This is the sort of trick you can perform anywhere, and the routine can last anywhere from five to fifteen minutes.

Let's assume that your partner is the mind reader. He stands at the front blindfolded or with his back to the audience. You pass among the group with a deck of cards. Someone touches a card, and your partner gradually names the card, with no apparent signal from you.

You and your partner can perfect the system in half an hour or so. Basic to the deception is this: You signal either by saying something, or by *saying nothing*. If you say, "All right," or "Right," you have given an *audible signal*. If you say nothing, you have given a *silent signal*.

Also misleading is the fact that you feed your partner the information a little at a time.

Here is the basic code:

NO SIGNAL	SIGNAL	EXTRA SIGNAL
Nothing	"All right" or "Right"	"Yes"

1. Red	Black	
2. Club or Heart	Spade or Diamond	
3. Low (2 to 7)	High (8 to King)	Ace
4. Odd (3, 5, 7 or 9, J, K)	Even (2, 4, 6 or 8, 10, Q)	
5. First of Group (3, 9, 2, or 8)	Second of Group (5, J, 4, or 10)	Third of Group (7, K, 6, or Q)

The chart isn't as complicated as it looks. Let's try an example. You spread the cards before a spectator, and he touches the nine of spades. First, you are to convey the color. The card is black, so signal by saying, "All right." Your partner sees dark clouds and declares the card is black.

You are working one category ahead. Now you must convey the precise suit. A spade or diamond requires a signal, so you say, "Right." Your partner already knows that the card is black, so divines that it is a spade.

You must now tell your partner whether the card is high or low. A nine is considered high, which calls for a signal. You say, "Right," and partner declares that it is a high card. Next comes odd or even. The nine of spades is obviously an odd card, so you must send no signal. You say nothing. Partner pauses a bit to make sure you are sending no signal, and then says that the card is odd.

At this point the mind reader knows that the card is a nine, jack, or king. For the first of the group, a nine, you would give no signal; for the second of the group, a jack, you would signal; for the third of the group, a king, you would give the extra signal, "Yes." Since it is the first of the group, you say nothing.

Your partner now reveals the full name of the card, the nine of spades.

When the card chosen is an ace, you first send the color, and then the suit. The next signal is the *extra signal,* "Yes." So the card is revealed very quickly.

The most puzzling part for most spectators is that you so often give no signal whatever.

Incidentally, make sure your partner likes to playact; an important part of the routine is that the mind reader convincingly pretends to gradually get the message from the spectator telepathically.

Make a copy of the chart for your partner and then, both using charts, practise sending various cards. Shortly, you will both be quite proficient and will no longer need your "cheatsheets."

♦ The Hindu Shuffle Force ♦

One of the best ways to "read a spectator's mind" is to force the selection of a particular card. The next four tricks provide excellent methods.

For most forces, you must know the top card. Here are some ways:

(1) In toying with the deck, glance at the bottom card. In an overhand shuffle, move it to the top.

(2) Fan through the cards to make sure the joker has been removed. Note the top card.

(3) This is probably the best method. Riffle-shuffle the cards

Illus. 12. When separating the cards before you riffle, you're bound to see the bottom card of at least one of the packets.

while standing up. In separating the cards before you riffle, you're bound to see the bottom card of at least one of the packets (Illus. 12). Perform a riffle shuffle, interweaving the corners of the cards, rather than the ends. Make sure the card you sighted is the bottom card of the deck at the conclusion of the shuffle. Give the cards an overhand shuffle, bringing the bottom card to the top.

Once you know the top card, you are ready to use *The Hindu Shuffle Force.* "Tell me where to stop," you say as you begin the Hindu Shuffle. As with the false *Hindu Shuffle,* draw off the first packet, and as a second packet is drawn off, the right second and third fingers and thumb pick up a portion of the packet just dropped. Continue drawing off *small* packets until the spectator says stop. Bring the pile in your right hand directly over the pile in your left hand and release the cards below the break. Thus, the top card you sighted is now the top card of the pile in your left hand.

Tap the rear end of the pile in your left hand with the cards in your right hand once or twice (Illus. 13), saying, "Take a look at your card." Extend the pile in your left hand towards the spectator. After he looks, replace the other cards on top and hand him the deck to shuffle. While he does so, gradually read his mind, revealing the color, the suit, the value.

Illus. 13. Tap the rear end of the pile in your left hand with the cards in your right hand.

♦ Up-And-Down Force ♦

This is similar to a trick in which a card is palmed behind the back. It's perfect for those who are hesitant to attempt even so discreet a palm.

Make sure there's no one behind you to observe the secret move you must perform. You must know the name of the top card.

Announcing that you are going to attempt a feat of telepathy, place the deck *face up* on the table. Ask a volunteer to cut off a huge pile of cards and turn them over on the rest of the deck. Then he is to cut off a smaller pile and turn it face up on the rest of the deck. He can continue cutting off smaller piles and turning them over on the deck a number of times.

"Pretty mixed up, I'd say," you declare. Pick up the cards and place them behind your back with your left hand as you turn away from the spectators. Your back is now to the group, cards behind your back in your left hand. "I want you to cut off a pile of cards, but please cut into the face-down cards so that no one else can see your choice."

After he has cut off a pile, turn back towards the spectators briefly, keeping the cards behind your back. Make sure your right hand is in front where the group can see it. Ask, "Did you cut into the face-down cards?" While saying this, stick your left thumb underneath the pile and flip the cards over (Illus. 14).

Illus. 14. Stick your left thumb underneath the pile and flip the cards over.

The spectator, of course, answers yes to your question. Immediately turn away again, telling your assistant, "Kindly look at the card you cut to. And show it to one other person. Now replace the card on top and put the rest of the cards on top of it." After he has done this, say, "Please take the deck into your hands and concentrate on your card."

Gradually read his mind.

◆ The Braue Force ◆

This trick is named for its inventor, Frederick Braue. It's an easy sleight and extremely useful. What's more, it's the most efficient way to secretly turn a card face up.

Here is the sleight: Hold the deck in the dealing position in your left hand. With your right thumb, raise the top card at the rear a fraction of an inch and hold a break with your thumb (Illus. 15). With the left hand take the bottom half of the deck to the left (Illus. 16). Flip these cards over with your

Illus. 15. With your right thumb, raise the top card at the rear a fraction of an inch and hold a break with your thumb.

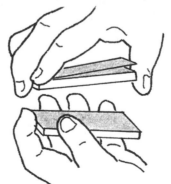

Illus. 16. With the left hand, take the bottom half of the deck to the left.

left thumb and place them face up on top. With the left hand take all the cards *below the break you are holding with your right thumb*, flip these over with your left thumb and place them face up on top. You are now holding the deck face up with a face-down card, which you know, at the back.

To do the force, you must know the name of the top card. Say to a volunteer, "You will select a card, and I will try to read your mind." As you cut the first packet and turn it face up on the deck, say, "You might choose this card." As you turn the second packet face up on the deck, say, "Or you might choose this one. Please cut off a large portion of the cards and shuffle them."

You extend your hand with the face-up cards and he cuts off a large packet. After he has shuffled them, ask him to cut the cards into three face-down piles, pointing out that three is a mystic number. "Which of the three piles do you choose?" You're holding a small packet face up in your left hand. Take them into your right hand and drop them, face up, onto the chosen pile. The card you peeked at is now the first of the face-down cards.

Immediately pick up one of the other piles and fan through them face up, cursorily glancing at the faces. Set the cards aside face down. "All right. I've mentally eliminated these." Pick up the other unselected pile and do the same thing, setting them face down on top of the first pile you examined.

"Hand me the face-up cards, please." The spectator gives you the face-up cards. You do the fanning business once more and add these to your discard pile. "Please look at the card you selected," you say, pointing to the top card of the remaining pile. "Since we have already eliminated most of the deck, it should be easy to get your telepathic message." He returns his card and shuffles the pile, concentrating first on the suit and then the value as you gradually read his mind.

◆   The Do-It-Yourself Force   ◆

For this force, you need to know the bottom card. Hand the deck to a spectator. Tell him to cut off a pile of cards and place it on the table. He turns the next card face up and places it on top of the pile he cut off. Now he puts the packet in his hands on top of the cards on the table.

"Pick up the deck, please," you say. "I want you to fan through the cards so that only you can see the faces. Fan to the card you turned over. The card right after that is your card. Kindly remember its name. Now turn the face-down card over and give the deck a good shuffle."

The spectator, of course, has noted the original bottom card of the deck, and you're ready to read his mind.

TIME FOR A CHANGE

Cards change places or invisibly leap from one place to another. This type of trick seems to be genuine magic and always pleases onlookers.

◆   Simple Exchange   ◆

You must know the name of the top card, your key card. A number of methods are given in *The Hindu Shuffle Force*, page 33. Hand the deck to a volunteer and then turn away. Say, "Think of a number from five to twenty and count that many, one on top of the other, face down on the table." When he finishes, say, "Set the rest of the deck aside. Turn over the last card you dealt. Let everybody have a look and then put it back."

Turn back to the group. Ask your assistant to give his packet three complete cuts. Take the pile and, as you speak, give it several quick overhand cuts, as though shuffling. "I want to find out if our minds are on the same track." Fan through the pile, faces towards yourself. Find the key card; the card on the near side of it is the one chosen. Pull this from the fan as though contemplating choosing it. Shake your head no, and replace it on the far side of the key card. Consider other cards. Finally, cut the key card to the bottom; this places the chosen card second from the bottom. Show the bottom card, holding the cards in the glide grip. Say, "Here's my choice." Name the card. "Does this happen to be your chosen card?" No. Turn the cards down and then glide the chosen card, placing it face down on the table. Place the pile on top of the deck. Now his card is on the table, and your card is at the chosen number down in the deck—minus one.

Pick up the deck. Remove the top and bottom cards and toss them onto the table face up. "Is either of these your card?" No. Pick them up and place them face down on top. Your card is now at the proper number from the top. "What was the number you thought of?" The spectator tells you. Count off that number from the top. Turn over the last card you deal. It is the one you chose, which you presumably placed on the table. "But that's *my* card. What's the name of your card?" He names it, and you turn over the card on the table.

"See? I was right in the first place."

◆ The Travelling Trio—1 ◆

This astonishing old trick is seldom performed nowadays, perhaps because the original version called for a rather cumbersome sleight. I have fashioned two versions, either of which makes the trick easier and more effective.

"We need three particular cards," you explain, as you turn the deck face up and run through the cards so that all can see. Find the ace of spades. Say, "The ace of spades." Separate the cards so that the ace is at the face of the cards in your left hand. Lift these cards above the others and, with your right thumb, pull the ace of spades onto the bottom of the deck.

Fan through the deck again and add the two of spades to the bottom of the deck in the same way, naming the card. Do the same with the three of spades. Even up the cards. As you hold the face-up deck in your hand, the three of spades is the uppermost card, and below it is the two, followed by the ace.

Make sure the deck is tilted downward so that all can see. Spread the bottom four cards to the right, lifting off the bottom three an inch or so with your right hand. As you do so, pull the bottom card back onto the deck with your left thumb, securing a break beneath it with your left little finger. "The ace, two, and three of spades," you say as you continue. Close the three cards against the base of your left thumb. Your right fingers naturally come under the card you have separated and add it to the bottom of the packet in your right hand. Move the four cards a few inches to the right of the deck. *As soon as your right hand clears the deck, you must turn your left hand over in a clockwise direction (Illus. 17), and place the deck face down on the table.* The reason is that you don't wish spectators to notice that the bottom card isn't the one it's supposed to be.

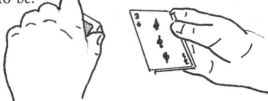

Illus. 17. As soon as your right hand clears the deck, you must turn your left hand over in a clockwise direction and place the deck face down on the table.

"We'll use these cards . . . " Casually gesture toward the face-down deck with the four cards. " . . . and we'll also use the rest of the deck." You're holding the packet of four cards with fingers beneath and thumb on top. Bring the cards down to the right side of the deck and nonchalantly flip them face down on top (Illus. 18). Without lifting the deck, straighten out the cards by patting the sides with both hands.

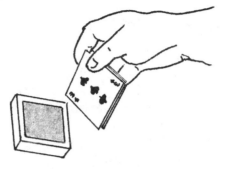

Illus. 18. Bring the cards down to the right side of the deck and nonchalantly flip them face down on top.

All of these moves are done smoothly, and without pause.

Now on top of the deck you have an extra card and below it, in order, the ace, two, and three of spades. With your right hand, pick off the top card and set it to the right of the deck, saying, "Ace." Pick off the next card and set it to the right of the first card, saying, "Two." Pick off the next card and set it to the right of the second card, saying, "Three."

"We'll start with the three," you continue. Pick up the deck with the right hand and drop it on top of the card on your right. (Actually, it is the two.) Rap the back of the deck with your right knuckles. Turn over the top card, showing that it is the three, and toss it face up to one side.

Pick up the original middle card. Set the deck down in its place. Put the card on top, saying, "Two." Again rap the back of the deck. Turn the deck over, showing that the two has penetrated to the bottom. Holding the deck face up, draw off the two and toss it near the three. You want everyone to see that an indifferent card is now on the bottom. For some reason, spectators find this compelling.

Place the deck on top of the last face-down card. Say, "Ace,"

and again rap with the knuckles. Turn over the top card, showing the ace.

♦ The Travelling Trio—2 ♦

This version takes a bit more time, but you may prefer it. Fan
through the deck so all can see. Find the three of spades and
place it *on top*. On top of that, place the two of spades. And
on top of all, place the ace of spades. Name each card as you
place it on top. Even up the cards and turn the deck face
down.

"You must remember the order," you say as you fan off the
top three cards and take them in your right hand. Push off the
next card with your left thumb and draw it back, obtaining a
little-finger break beneath it. Close up the cards in your right
hand against the base of your left thumb, letting the right
fingers slide under the fourth card, adding it to your stack.
Holding the cards in your right hand, set the deck down.

Turn over the top card, saying, "First the ace." Turn the
card face down and place it on the bottom. Do the same with
the two and the three. Drop the four cards on top of the deck
and proceed as with the first version.

♦ The Known Leaper ♦

Have a volunteer shuffle the cards. Rapidly deal the cards into
a pile in this manner: Deal the first card face down, saying,
"One." Deal the next face up. Deal the third face down, saying,
"Two." Deal the next face up. Continue in this manner until
you deal the fifth face-down card, saying, "Five." Pause and
say, "Yours are the face-down cards. Mine are the face-up ones.
Stop me on any face-down card."

You begin dealing again, but there is a subtle—and most
important—change in the rhythm. You deal the next card face

up, saying nothing. Deal the next face down, saying, "Six." Continue alternating until the spectator stops you at a face-down card. Suppose he stops you at the count of 11. Tell him to look at the card, show it around, and replace it on the pile.

"Number eleven," you say to make sure everyone remembers. Deal several more face-up and face-down cards, saying, "You could have gone as far as you wanted and chosen any card you wished." You can end the deal on either a face-up or face-down card.

Stop dealing. Pick up the cards on the table with your right hand and place them on the deck, as though straightening them. Fan quickly through to the last face-up card and take these cards off. Set the rest of the deck aside. You have now removed the bottom card from the pile (number one) and arranged it so that his card will now be at number ten, rather than eleven.

"Let's get these cards back in order." One at a time, deal the face-down cards in front of your helper, and the face-up ones in front of you. As you deal yours, however, turn each face-up card face down.

Make some "mystic waves" over the two piles. "That should do it. Now let's go down to your number. First I'll take one from my pile, and then you hand me one from yours."

With your right hand, take the top card from your pile and place it in your left hand in the glide grip, saying, "One." He hands you his top card and you place it *beneath* the card in your left hand. Place your next card beneath the others in your left hand, saying, "Two." When he hands you his next card, place it beneath the others. Continue until you reach the spectator's number, in our example, eleven. The bottom card of the pile in your hand is the chosen card. Say, "Eleven," pick up the top card of your pile on the table, and add it to the bottom of those in your hand. "Hold it! That's your number. Turn over your card, please."

As he turns over his card, casually perform the glide. Move your right hand forward with the card so that it is near the pile on the table. "Not your card, right?" He agrees. "What was it again?" When he names it, turn over the card in your hand and drop it face up on your pile, saying, "No, not in your pile; in *my* pile."

◆   I Love the Piano   ◆

From the deck count off eight cards into a pile, and say, "Eight cards—an even number." Count off eight into another pile and say the same thing. Ask a volunteer to place his hands on the table in a piano-playing position, fingertips under, and touching the table (Illus. 19).

You'll now stick a pair of cards in each available space in both hands. There is space in each hand for eight cards (Illus. 20). As you place each pair between the fingers, comment, "Two, an even number."

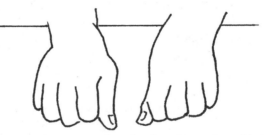

Illus. 19. Ask a volunteer to place his hands on the table in a piano-playing position, fingertips under, and touching the table.

Take one pair from between the spectator's fingers, saying, "An even number." Separate them so that you are holding one in each hand. Drop them next to each other on the table. Take another pair and follow exactly the same procedure, placing these on top of the other two on the table. Continue until only one pair remains between your helper's fingers. On the table are two piles with seven cards in each.

Take the last two cards, once more saying, "An even num-

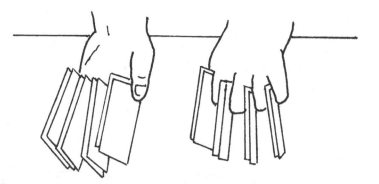

Illus. 20. Now stick a pair of cards in each available space in both hands.

ber." Ask the spectator to choose a pile. Drop the two on top of this pile, again saying, "An even number."

Take one card off the deck and place it on top of the other pile, saying, "And we'll make this one an odd number." Pause. "Now, before your very eyes, I will magically transfer a card from the odd pile to the even pile."

Snap your fingers. Count the pile to which you added a card from the top of the deck. Eight cards; it is now even. Count the other pile. Nine cards; it is now odd.

♦ The Sheep and the Robbers ♦

Fan through the cards, tossing out—face up—two jacks, five spot cards, and a king.

"These two jacks are robbers," you explain. "They came to a farmhouse one evening . . . " Tap the deck, indicating that this is the farmhouse. " . . . and asked the farmer if they could stay there overnight." Point to the king, saying, "This is the farmer. He said, 'I have two empty barns . . .' " Pull out your side trouser pockets, showing that they are empty. " ' . . . and you can each sleep in one of them. But I have five sheep in the barnyard, and I don't want you stealing them.' "

Gesture towards the face-up spot cards. Pick them up and hold them in your left hand in a face-down pile. Deal them into a face-down row from left to right.

"So the farmer went into the house and went to bed." Place the king on top of the deck. "And each of the robbers went into a barn." Take the jacks, one in each hand, and place them face inward into your side trouser pockets.

"But robbers will be robbers. So they soon stole the sheep one by one."

With the right hand, take the spot card on the right and put it into your right pocket under the jack—that is, closer to your body. With your left hand, take the spot card on the left and put it into your left pocket the same way. With your right hand, take the spot card now on the right and place it into the pocket under the others.

In your right pocket are four cards, jack on top; in the left pocket are three cards, jack on top.

"The farmer woke up in the middle of the night and wondered if his sheep were safe." Turn the king over on top of the deck. "He turned on a light and headed for the door. The minute the robbers saw the light, they knew they had better put the sheep back. So they returned them one by one."

Now take five cards from your pockets and place them face down on the table, like this:

(1) Take the jack from your *left* pocket and place it face down to your left.

(2) Take the jack from your *right* pocket and place it face down to the right of the first jack.

(3) Alternately take three spot cards from the left and right pockets, placing them in turn face down to the right of the others.

Pick up the king, saying, "The farmer saw that everything was as it should be, so he returned to the house." Place the king face down on top of the deck.

"But the robbers were not satisfied with their close call. They *wanted* those sheep. So what did they do?" Pause for a response. "Lucky guess. That's right, they stole the sheep again."

Laid out on the table from left to right are two jacks and three spot cards. Alternately place the cards in your pockets, starting with the card at the right with your right hand. You now have five spot cards in your right pocket and the two jacks in your left pocket.

"But the farmer sensed that something funny was going on." Take the king from the top of the deck and drop it face up on the table. "He got out of bed without turning on the light. Then he grabbed his shotgun, went into the barnyard, and discovered that his sheep were missing. The robbers were in big trouble. Only one thing could save them: if the sheep were in one barn . . . " Take the five spot cards from your right pocket and spread them face up on the table. " . . . and the robbers were in the other." Take the two jacks from your left pocket and drop them face up on the table.

"And, of course, there was nothing else in the barns." Pull out your pockets, showing that they're empty.

A woman who wants to perform this trick may not have the available pockets. She could wear her coat if it has pockets, or she could borrow a man's suit jacket and use the side pockets. Either way adds amusement to the trick.

◆ The Joiners ◆

A spectator shuffles the deck, cuts it into two parts, and gives you one.

"We will each choose a card, look at it, and put it on top," you say. The spectator does so. You, on the other hand, tilt your portion forward as you look for an appropriate card (Illus. 21). In doing so, peek at the bottom card and remember it. Take any card from the middle, look at it, and place it on top. But, of course, you disregard this card.

Place your pile on the table, and invite your volunteer to

Illus. 21. Tilt your portion forward as you look for an appropriate card.

do likewise with his pile. Say, "Place either pile on top of the other, and then give the cards three complete cuts."

When he finishes, say, "My card was . . . " Name the card you peeked at. "What was yours?" He names his card. Repeat the names of the two cards. Tap the deck. Pick it up and fan through, showing the cards. A miracle—the two cards are together in the deck.

DISCOVERY

A card is chosen, and the magician locates it—the simplest kind of card trick. This is the basic theme of some of the most imaginative card tricks you can perform.

◆ Cards from Pocket ◆

This is a simple but effective trick . . . if you have mastered the *Hindu Shuffle* (page 7).

Have four cards chosen by different spectators. Collect the cards from left to right. Draw off a packet from the top with your left hand in the first movement of the *Hindu Shuffle*. Extend the packet towards the farthest person on the left who chose a card, telling him to replace his card on top. Bring the pile in your right hand over the other pile and continue the *Hindu Shuffle*, bringing the chosen card to the top.

Moving to the right, have the next spectator replace his card in the same way, and bring it to the top above the first chosen card. Repeat this with the remaining spectators who chose cards. The cards are now on top in reverse order of their return. Place the deck in your pocket. With thumb and first finger, separate the top four cards. "Whose card first?" you ask.

Whichever spectator volunteers, you instantly bring out his card and present it to him. Repeat for the others who chose a card.

♦ **Jacks Be Nimble** ♦

Start by taking the jack of hearts and the jack of spades from the deck and tossing them face up on the table. "Here we have the one-eyed jacks, and they have most peculiar properties, as you will see."

Remove a card from the deck and, without showing its face, place it on top of one of the face-up jacks, and place the other face-up jack on top of both. Explain: "Place a card between the jacks and what do we have? Right. A one-eyed-jack sandwich."

Spread the deck for the selection of a card. Tell the spectator to look at his card and set it down for a moment. Pick up the jack sandwich and place it on top of the deck, saying, "Let's get rid of the jack sandwich." Give the cards a complete cut.

"Yes, we really do have the jack sandwich in the middle." Fan through the cards to show the jack sandwich. As you close up the deck, obtain a break below the uppermost jack with the little finger of your left hand. Transfer the break to your right thumb and perform *The Triple-Cut Control* (see page 10).

You now have a face-up jack on the bottom, an indifferent card face down on top, and a face-up jack second from the top. Place the deck on top of the spectator's card, saying, "Did everyone see the selected card? No?"

Pick up the deck and turn it over, holding it face up in your left hand. As you display the chosen card, name it. "Now," you say to your volunteer, "I want you to pick the exact point at which I should cut the deck."

This is where you get rid of that extra card on top, the one nearest your left palm. Tilt the deck downward and then carefully draw the card away with your right hand. Your best bet is to hold the deck high in your left hand at the tips of fingers and thumb, and carefully draw the card *away from you* (Illus. 22). Hand it to the spectator. "Stick it partway into the deck, anywhere you want."

Illus. 22. Hold the deck high in your left hand at the tips of fingers and thumb, and carefully draw the card away from you.

Wherever he sticks it, meticulously cut the face-up cards so that his inserted card becomes the card on the face of the deck. Straighten up the cards and set the deck on the table face down.

"In the deck we have your chosen card and jack sandwich. Let's take a look and see if the card in the jack sandwich can tell us anything about your card."

Fan through the face-down cards and remove the jack sandwich. Turn it over, showing the selected card between the jacks. "See how smart I was? I picked *your* card to put into the jack sandwich."

◆ Quick Location ◆

A card is selected, and you bring it fourth from the top. When you spread the deck for the return of the card, fan out three cards above it, and secure a little-finger break at that point. Thus, you can perform *The Triple Cut Control* (see page 10), bringing the card to fourth from the top.

After the chosen card is brought into position, spread the deck face down on the table, requesting the spectator to take out any card and turn it face up. "It will locate your card," you say.

You gather up the deck, and proceed to spell out the value of this card to locate the chosen card, dealing off one card from the top for each letter in the spelling. The secret is simple. *All* cards (considering the values, not suits) can be spelled out in three, four, or five letters. *Ace*, for example, spells out in three letters. *Eight* spells out in five letters.

With three-letter cards, you spell out the value and turn over the next card. With four-letter cards, you spell out the value and turn over the last card of the spelling. With five-letter cards, you call attention to the value of the card and place it face down on top. Then you spell out the value and turn over the last card of the spelling.

◆ What's the Difference? ◆

A card is chosen, shown around, and returned to the deck. You bring it to the top. Ask a spectator to give you a number from one to ten. Deal that many into a face-down pile. Turn over the next card, asking, "Is this the chosen card?" It is not. Replace the card, and place the others on top of the deck.

Ask a second spectator to give you a number from ten to twenty. Deal that many into a face-down pile, turn over the next card, again asking if it is the chosen one. Again you're wrong. Once more replace the card, and place the others on top.

"Maybe three is the charm," you say, handing the deck to a spectator. Have him subtract the first chosen number from the second chosen number. He takes the result and deals that many face-down on the table. Ask the name of the selected card. Have the next card turned over. At last you succeed.

◆ About Face ◆

One of the most astonishing of effects is the discovery of a chosen card face up in the middle of the deck.

Have a spectator select a card, show it around and return it to the deck. You bring it to the top with *The Hindu Shuffle* (page 7) or *The Triple-Cut Control* (page 10). Then you perform the turnover, described in *The Braue Force*, page 36. As you turn each of the two packets face up, you ask, "Does this happen to be your card?" At this point, the deck is face up and the chosen card is reversed at the back.

You now cut the face-up cards by drawing out the lower half towards you and placing it on top. You may instead do a *Hindu Shuffle* (see page 7), drawing off small packets, and then dropping about half on top. Ask if he has seen his card. He has not. Turn the deck face down. "We'll just have to try magic."

Tap the deck and then either fan the cards out or spread them on the table, showing the chosen card face up in the middle.

◆ Gentle Persuasion ◆

Fan through the cards face down, offering the selection of a card. As you pass the cards from hand to hand, count off the top seven in two groups of three plus one card. Hold them

slightly apart from the rest. After the card is chosen, close up
the deck, securing a little-finger break beneath the seven cards.
The deck is in your left hand in the dealing position, while
the right hand grips the ends from above. Transfer the little-
finger break to the right thumb. Run your *left* thumb halfway
down the side of the deck, riffling the cards, and then lift off
the seven cards (Illus. 23). The illusion is that you casually

*Illus. 23. Run your left thumb halfway down the side of the deck,
riffling the cards, and then lift off the seven cards.*

riffled to the middle of the deck. Offer the lower portion with
your left hand for the return of the card. His card is now
eighth from the top. Promptly give the deck a *False Hindu
Shuffle* (see page 9) or a false cut, making sure the top eight
cards remain undisturbed.

Casually deal five cards into a pile at a fairly slow rate. As
you deal the fifth card, say to the spectator, "Tell me when to
stop."

Pick up the pace a bit as you start a pile to the right of the
first. If all goes well, the spectator will tell you to stop when
you're holding his card, about to deal it as a third card on the
second pile. Ask him to name his card. You show the card.
It's a miracle!

Actually, there is quite a bit of leeway. If, for example, you
have just dealt down the sixth card and are stopped when
holding the seventh in your hand, simply place the seventh
card on the pile and show the present top card of the deck.

If you have already dealt the eighth card down and are stopped when holding the ninth, simply return the card in your hand to the top of the deck and turn over the card you just dealt off.

After you've tried the trick a dozen or so times, you'll develop a feel for it that will bring success the vast majority of the time. How about the rest of the time? No need for you to *ever* fail, and you will have plenty of practice on the timing while still performing successfully.

When a stubborn spectator keeps you dealing interminably, you can use my application of the *principle of 6 and 8*. This will cover you up to the 23rd card from the top. I never get that far, because when I reach the 17th card, I get another spectator to call for a stop.

You have dealt a 5-card pile and, to the right of it, a 3-card pile, the top card of which is the chosen one. To the right of that, you deal a 2-card pile. After this, you deal small piles at random. When the spectator says stop, you set the deck down. Shortly, you will gather up the piles and have the spectator perform an elimination deal.

It is vital that you keep track of the number of cards you deal. Divide the final number by two, casting off the remainder of one if need be. If the result is *even*, the selected card must be placed sixth from the top in the stack you give the spectator. If the result is *odd*, the selected card must be placed eighth from the top.

Suppose the result is even. Place the first pile you dealt—the 5-card pile—on top of the second pile, which has the chosen card on top. All other piles go on the bottom. The chosen card is sixth from the top.

If the result is odd, place both the first pile (5 cards) and the third pile (2 cards) on top of the second pile. All other piles go on the bottom. The chosen card is eighth from the top.

Hand the packet to the spectator with these instructions: "Deal the top card onto the deck and the next one onto the table. Keep doing this until you run out of cards. Then pick up the cards on the table and do the same thing: first card on the deck, next on the table, and so on."

He is to repeat the dealing procedure until only one card remains. It is the chosen one.

♦ Any Number ♦

Here is a quick trick that provides an excellent effect with little effort.

You must bring a selected card to seventh from the top of the deck. The procedure is identical with the replacement of a card in *Gentle Persuasion*, except in this instance you hold six cards separate so that the chosen card becomes seventh from the top.

Say to your volunteer, "Give me a number between five and ten." The phrasing restricts his choices to six, seven, eight, and nine." If he says six, deal off six cards one at a time and place the next card aside. If he says seven, deal off seven cards and place the last card aside. If he says eight, deal the cards by twos onto the table, one pair on top of the other. "Two, four, six, eight." Take the top card of those dealt and place it aside. If he says nine, deal the cards in groups of three, saying, "Three, six, nine." Take the top card of those dealt and place it aside.

In each instance you have set aside the original seventh card from the top. The spectator names his card, and you turn it face up.

♦ Spelling Counts—1 ♦

A card is chosen and replaced 18th from the top. You use the same technique as mentioned in the two previous tricks. False shuffle or false cut, retaining the order of at least the top 18 cards.

You now ask, "Is your card odd or even?" According to the answer, spell out *odd* or *even*, dealing one card from the top into a pile for every letter in the spelling. Ask if it is a face card or a spot card. Spell out *face* or *spot*. Do the same for *red* or *black*.

Now ask for the suit. Here is how you handle clubs, spades, hearts, or diamonds. However the spectator gives the suit, repeat it as *clubs, spade, or diamond*. Then spell it exactly that way.

Now ask for the suit. Here is how you handle clubs, spades, or diamonds. However the spectator gives the suit, repeat it as *clubs, spade, or diamond*. Then spell it exactly that way.

Ask the spectator the name of the chosen card. If you spelled out *odd* at the beginning, turn over the next card. If you spelled out *even*, turn over the last card of the spelling.

Hearts are treated differently. If it is an even heart, you spell out *hearts*, and turn over the next card. An odd heart requires special handling. You have already been told that you have a *red odd* card. (*Spot* or *face*, of course, is irrelevant.) When the spectator says that his suit is hearts, say, "I believe I have your card right here." Turn over the top card. You are wrong. Bury the card in the middle. "All right, then. What did you say your suit was?" He names it again. You say, "Hearts," and spell it out, turning over the next card after the spelling.

◆ Spelling Counts—2 (Easy) ◆

Have the spectator shuffle the cards and deal the entire deck into three piles. There are 18 cards in the first pile and 17 cards in each of the others. The spectator is to pick out a pile, shuffle it, look at the top card, and place the pile down. At least one of the other piles must have 17 cards in it. Direct him to pick up that pile, shuffle it and place it on top of the one with his chosen card on top. While he is doing this, grasp the other pile at the sides and draw it towards you. Pick it up and tap the sides on the table. As you do so, peek at the bottom card. If you wish, shuffle the pile, retaining the bottom card. Place the pile on top of the combined pile on the table.

Tell your assistant to give the cards several complete cuts.

"Now this is really clever," you say. Fan through the deck, find the key card, and cut it to the bottom. Display the card. "*This*," you declare dramatically, "is not your card!"

The audience is not impressed. "Maybe we should try something else."

Since the chosen card is now in position, you can proceed with the spelling as in the original version.

◆ The Rising Card ◆

A card is chosen, returned, and brought to the top. Hold the deck between fingertips and thumb and lift it so that the face of the deck is towards the audience (Illus. 24).

Rub your right forefinger against your sleeve, saying that you are trying to create a "magnetic field." Place the finger on top of the deck and lift it, trying to draw the chosen card from the deck (Illus. 25). Repeat this maneuver a few times.

Illus. 24. Hold the deck between fingertips and thumb and lift it so that the face of the deck is towards the audience.

Then place the first finger on top of the deck and extend your little finger, pressing it against the top card. This time when you raise your finger, the pressure of the little finger causes the top card to rise (Illus. 26). After the card has risen

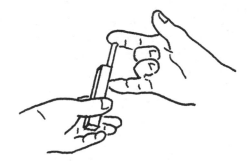

Illus. 26. When you raise your finger, the pressure of the little finger causes the top card to rise.

Illus. 25. Place the fingers on top of the deck, and lift it, trying to draw the chosen card from the deck.

about halfway, grasp it between the first finger and thumb. Fold in the little finger. Hand the card to the spectator who chose it.

♦ The Rising Card Deluxe ♦

Up to a point, this is the same effect as the previous trick. A chosen card is brought to the top of the deck. With the right thumb at the rear of the deck, you separate the two top cards and hold the break with your left little finger.

As with *The Rising Card*, you attempt to create a "magnetic field" and repeatedly try to draw the card from the deck with your right first finger. At last you get the card to rise. You extend the little finger so that it goes under the deck and pulls back the top two cards about 1/2″ (Illus. 27). The two are raised about half the length of the deck. The double card is held in place by the left thumb and fingers as you grasp it at the top

Illus. 27. Extend the little finger so that it goes under the deck and pulls back the top two cards about 1/2".

Illus. 28. Display the double card.

with the right fingers and thumb. Display the double card (Illus. 28). Set it face down on top of the deck.

"Your chosen card," you say, "magically risen from the deck." Deal the top card face down on the table. When the spectator denies this, ask the name of his card. Have him turn over the card on the table. "I knew I was right."

♦ Thirty-Three—1 ♦

You will need a complete deck of 52 cards. Say, "I would like to try an experiment to see if some of you ladies and gentlemen can locate a selected card."

Have a card selected, shown around, and returned to the deck. Bring it to the bottom with *The Triple-Cut Control* (see page 10). Give the deck a false shuffle, keeping the card at the bottom.

Ask for three assistants, although you can have one person do all the work, if you wish. Count off *eleven* cards from the top and hand them to assistant one. The best way to do this is to take the cards one under the other, counting them in threes, thus: three, six, nine, plus two.

Say, "Shuffle these cards a bit and then take one out and set it down on the table face up."

When he finishes, take the rest of the cards from him and put them on the bottom of the deck. Count off ten cards from the top in the same way as before and hand them to assistant two. Make the same request as you did of assistant one.

When he finishes, take the cards back and place them on the bottom of the deck. At this point, the chosen card is 33rd from the top of the deck.

Thumb off a pile comparable to the other two. Make the action look like your previous counts, but pay little attention, creating the impression that the other piles were created with the same indifference. Give this pile to assistant three. Once more, the spectator is to mix the cards, choose one, and place it on the table face up. Take back the pile and place it *on top of the deck.*

Hand the deck to the first assistant, asking him to count enough cards face down on top of his card to bring the total to ten. (Aces count as one, and face cards count as ten.) For example, if the face-up card is a six, the spectator would deal four cards onto it, saying, "Seven, eight, nine, ten." Make sure that enough of the face-up card is exposed so that the value can be seen. Have each of the other two assistants perform the same duty.

Select one of your assistants and say to him, "You look like a mathematical wizard. Would you please add up the value of the three face-up cards and count off that many from the top of the deck."

Ask the name of the chosen card and turn over the last card

counted off. Be sure to compliment the spectators for performing such an extraordinary trick for you.

◆ **Thirty-Three—2 (Easy)** ◆

You don't start by having a card chosen. Instead, hand out eleven cards to an assistant, asking him to mix them and take one out and place it on the table face up. *Immediately*, hand ten cards to a second spectator, giving the same instructions. As with the first version, casually fan off a comparable number and give them to a third spectator, asking him to do the same as the others. *And hand the rest of the deck to a fourth spectator*, giving him the same directions.

Take back the cards from spectators one and two, holding them in a pile. "Oh, we'd better have a card selected. Which one of these face-up cards shall we choose?" Pick up the card selected by the audience and name it, so that all will remember which one was chosen. Place it on top of the pile in your hand. Casually put the other two piles on top of the deck.

Proceed to the end of the trick, as in the other version.

◆ **Lucky Seven** ◆

Start by discussing how lucky the number seven is, and then ask a spectator to do a trick for you. Hand him a deck of cards and turn away.

Say, "Please shuffle the cards, and then count off seven and set the rest of the deck aside. Look at the top card and show it around." After he has done so, continue: "Think of any number from one to ten. Transfer that many from top to bottom, one card at a time."

Turn back, take the seven cards, and place them behind your back. Reverse their order by taking them one on top of the other into the right hand. Patter about having to hold the cards behind your back for exactly seven seconds to make the experiment work.

"Time's up," you declare, bringing the cards forward. Hand them to your assistant. Turn away again. Say, "Please transfer the same number from top to bottom as you did before." The chosen card is now on the bottom. Turn back and tell the spectator to place the top card on the bottom, the next on the table, the next on the bottom, and so on. When he has one card left, stop him, saying, "What is your card?" He turns it over, and that's it!

♦ Houdini Knows ♦

Give a spectator the deck and turn away, telling him to shuffle the cards thoroughly. Say, "We need a fairly large number of cards, so think of a number from twenty to twenty-nine. Count off that number onto the table. Keep it quiet so that I can't tell the number." Pause. "Pick up the cards you just counted off. Now add the digits in the number you selected, and count that many back onto the deck. For example, if you thought of 27, you would add the two and the seven, giving you nine. You count nine cards back on top of the deck. Do it very quietly."

After he finishes, continue: "Now set the deck aside; we won't be using it anymore. Take a small number of cards from your packet and put them into your pocket. It could be any number up to, say, eight." Pause. "Look at the card that lies at that number from the top, show it around, and leave it at that number from the top. For instance, if you put five cards in your pocket, you would look at the fifth card from the top and leave it at that number."

When he is done, turn back, take the packet, and say, "Why have we gone through all this? To make sure you have chosen a card at random and that there is no way I can know where it is. To make the feat even more difficult, I'm going to mix the cards a bit."

You move ten cards from the top to the bottom of the packet. The cards are moved in small groups. For example, you might spread the top several cards, take two of them, and place them on the bottom. In the same way, transfer three. Then one. Then two. Then two more. The total: ten. It doesn't matter how many you move each time, just so the total is ten. Don't worry about neatness; the sloppier, the better.

After you have transferred the cards, say, "Remember, you shuffled the deck before we began, and I have no way of knowing how many cards you put into your pocket. In other words, there is no way that anyone in the world could find your card. So let's try someone who is out of this world, the greatest magician of all time, Houdini. We will call on the spirit of the great Houdini by spelling out his name, like this . . . "

Spell out H-O-U-D-I-N-I, dealing one card off the top of the deck for each letter in the spelling. Then lift off the next card and ask the spectator to name his card. Turn the chosen card over, showing that, indeed, Houdini was kind enough to help out.

If the spectator fails to follow your directions, you will end up with the wrong card. Simply say, "Thanks a lot, Houdini," and go into your next trick.

♦ The No-Way Location ♦

While your back is turned, a spectator shuffles the deck, chooses a card, shuffles the deck again, and cuts the cards. You take the deck, thumb through the cards, and toss him his selected card.

You need a volunteer who knows how to riffle-shuffle. Hand him the deck, turn your back, and give the following instructions: "Please shuffle the cards thoroughly. When you're ready, cut the deck into three piles approximately even." Wait. "Now pick out one pile and shuffle it. Look at the top card of that pile, show it around, and return it to the top of that pile. Turn that pile face up and place it face up on top of one of the other two piles. You have a small face-down pile left. Place that face down on top of the rest of the cards."

When he is ready, say, "Please separate the deck around the middle and give the cards one good riffle shuffle." Pause. "Give the deck a complete cut. If anyone else wants to, he or she may also give the deck a complete cut."

Face the group, take the deck, and turn it over. Fan through the clumps of face-up and face-down cards. One string of face-up cards will be longer than any other. The first face-down card after this string is the selected card. Reveal it any way you wish.

I like to cut the cards, bringing the selected card to the top of the deck. I then fan through the deck, turning all the face-up cards face down. When I am done, I set the deck down, selected card on top, and declare, "There we are! All the cards now face the same way." Invariably, someone asks about the selected card. "Oh, yes, I almost forgot." I ask the name of the chosen card and turn it face up.

Sometimes the longest string of face-up cards will begin near the top of the deck and continue from the bottom up. This, of course, is caused by the cuts made by the spectators.

Occasionally when you fan through the cards, you will notice that more cards are face down than face up. This means that your assistant handed you the deck wrong-side up. Just turn the cards over and proceed.

♦   **A Good Indication**   ♦

This is a superior trick in which the spectator does all the work. You need a complete deck of 52 cards.

Turn your back and have a spectator shuffle the deck and then deal the cards into four equal piles. He pushes two of the piles to one side. "Now pick up one of the remaining piles," you instruct, "and pick out a card. Show it around, put it on top of the pile in your hands, and then put the pile on the table." Pause. "Cut off part of the other pile and place that bunch on top of your card. Now place the rest of that pile on top of the pile you have your card in."

The spectator's card is now 14th from the top. "We will have to find a magic indicator card," you say. "Deal the cards face up on the table one at a time, naming each one as you place it down. Don't go too fast now."

As he deals the first card, you mentally say, "Thirteen." When he deals the next, you think, "Twelve." You continue counting down until he hits a card that has the same number value as the one you are thinking. Stop him immediately. "That's it!" you say. Name the number value. "Please count that number from the top of the deck face down onto the table." Turn around and ask the name of the chosen card. Have him turn over the last card he dealt off. It's the selected card.

Remember that a king counts as 13, a queen as 12, and a jack as 11.

When you count backwards from 13, you actually have two chances on each number. Suppose the spectator says, "Seven of clubs," and you are thinking the number eight. Stop the spectator and have him deal off seven cards. When you turn around, you have him turn over *the next card* of the pile in his hand.

If you don't get a matching number, simply stop him after you count "one." Turn around, have him name the selected card, and then turn over the next card. You might say, "That's a pretty good indication," or, "I guess that's magic enough."

♦ The "Milking" Trick ♦

This is a modification of a trick invented by Alex Elmsley and revised by Stewart Judah.

Turn your back and ask a spectator to quietly deal two piles of cards with the same number in each pile. He can have, say, ten to twenty cards in each pile. "Set the rest of the deck aside," you say. "We won't be using it. Now look at the top card of one of the piles and remember it. Pick up the other pile. Take a small number of cards from that pile and place them on top of your chosen card. Hide the pile you're holding."

Turn around and pick up the packet containing the spectator's card. "We must give the packet a mystical double-card shuffle," you explain. Grip the cards from above with the left hand, thumb at the inner end, fingers at the outer end. Begin "milking" the cards into a single pile. That is, remove a card from the top and bottom at the same time with the thumb and fingers of the right hand and drop them into a pile (Illus. 29). Continue until all the cards are dealt this way. If one card remains, place it on top.

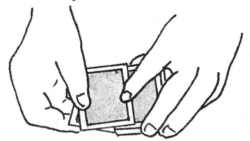

Illus. 29. Remove a card from the top and bottom at the same time with the thumb and fingers of the right hand and drop them into a pile.

Pick up the pile and toss out the bottom and top cards face up. "Neither of these is your card, right?" You are right. Place both cards face down on top of the packet. You have managed to add an additional card to the top of the packet.

Point out that you have no way of knowing how many cards the spectator has concealed. Ask him to take these cards and deal them into a pile as you deal yours into a separate pile. You deal card for card from your packet as he deals his cards. When he deals his last card, turn over the card you are dealing. It is the chosen one.

♦ What's the Name of That Card? ♦

I invented this trick some 45 years ago. This trick creates the impression that you have a magnificent memory. In fact, a good way to start is to tell the audience that you have a magnificent memory. "A glance through a deck of cards," you continue, "and I can tell you which card is missing."

Make sure you have a complete deck. Hand a volunteer the deck and ask him to shuffle. Tell him to remove one card of each suit, but not to choose face cards because even you have trouble with those. He places the cards face down on the table. Ask another spectator to pick one of the cards and put it in his pocket. While he does so, you casually add the other three to the bottom of the pack. If you wish, perform a riffle shuffle, keeping the three on the bottom.

Begin fanning through the cards, faces towards you. Note the bottom three cards; the missing suit is that of the chosen card. Rapidly count all the spot cards of this suit. Subtract the total from 55, and you have the value. Name the card, and have the spectator take the card from his pocket and display it.

♦ Ups and Downs ♦

This stunt is absurdly simple, but quite intriguing. Make sure you have a complete deck of 52 cards.

Bring the chosen card to the top and riffle-shuffle the deck, leaving it there. You're now going to deal the cards alternately into two piles; one pile will be face up, the other face down. Make sure you deal the first card face down. "Tell me when you see your card," you say to the spectator. When finished, push the face-up cards to one side, and instantly begin dealing two similar piles with the remaining 26 cards, this time starting with a face-up card.

You will make six such deals in all, each time discarding the face-up cards. The first card will be placed face down every time except the *second* time and the *last* time (when you deal two cards). The last face-down card will be the chosen one.

♦ The Numbers Game ♦

Give a spectator the deck. Turn away and say, "Think of a number from one to ten and look at the card that lies at that number from the top. Remember the number and the card, and keep the card at that number."

Turn back, take the deck, and ask a second spectator to give you a number from 10 to 20. Put the cards behind your back, saying, "I am going to bring the selected card to the new number."

Behind your back, quietly deal into your right hand, one on top of the other, a number of cards equal to the number given by the second spectator. Replace these on top. Suppose the second spectator said 16. You would reverse the order of the top 16 cards.

Bring the deck forward. Ask the first spectator what his number was. Let's say he says eight. Ask spectator two the same question. Once more he says 16. You say, "So we have the number eight." Pause, and then start dealing off the cards into a pile. With the first card, say, "Eight." With the second, say, "Nine." Continue to 16. The card at number 16 is the chosen one.

◆ What's in a Name? ◆

While your back is turned, a spectator shuffles the deck, then thinks of a number from five to fifteen. He looks at the card at that number from the top, keeping the deck in the same order. He remembers both the card and the number.

Take the deck and place it behind your back. Now transfer from the bottom to the top the same number of letters as are in your helper's name. The easiest way to do this is to turn the deck over and, from the face-up cards, deal out the proper number of cards into your right hand, taking one card under the other. As you deal, mentally spell out the name. Place these cards below those in your left hand. Turn the deck over.

You're all set, so bring the deck forward, saying, "I have moved your card from its original number. What number did you think of?" Count off that number of cards onto the table. Show that the last card dealt is not the spectator's card and replace it face down on the packet on the table. Drop the deck on top of the cards on the table.

"Please pick up the deck and spell out your name, dealing one card from the top for each letter in your name." When he finishes dealing, ask the name of the selected card. Have him turn over the last card he dealt.

◆ Upsy-Daisy ◆

A card is chosen, replaced, and brought second from the top. When the chosen card is returned, you can secure a little-finger break one card above it and perform *The Triple-Cut Control* (see page 10), or you might try this:

After the card is chosen, hold the deck in your left hand, with your right hand lightly gripping the ends of the top card (Illus. 30). With your left thumb, riffle down the side of the deck to about the middle. Tilt the deck forward, lifting off the top card with your right hand. Offer the rest of the deck

Illus. 30. (left) Hold the deck in your left hand, with your right hand lightly gripping the ends of the top card.

Illus. 31. (right) Tilt the deck forward, lifting off the top card with your right hand.

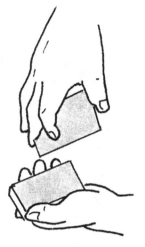

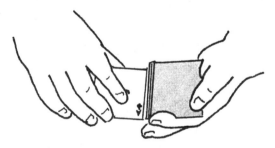

Illus. 32. (above) Holding the two top cards from above at the ends, take them as one and place them underneath the pile.

for the spectator to place his card on top (Illus. 31). Slap the card in your right hand back on top of the deck. The illusion is that the spectator replaced his card in the middle.

So the chosen card is second from the top. You fan out four

cards from the top and hold them about six inches to the right of the deck. Say, "Four cards," for those who aren't really bright with numbers. Meanwhile, push off the top card slightly with the left thumb, obtaining a slight little-finger break beneath it. As you close up the four cards against the base of your left thumb, your right fingers naturally come under the card you have separated and add it to the bottom of the stack. *Immediately* drop the left hand and set the rest of the deck aside.

Take off the top card of the five cards (presumably four) and turn it face up, holding it to the right of the deck. As above, secure a little-finger break under the top card (the one chosen). Replace the card face up on top of the other four and even the cards up at the ends with the right thumb and fingers. Ask, "Is this your card?" No.

Holding the two top cards from above at the ends, take them as one and place them underneath the pile (Illus. 32). Presumably, you have placed the top card face up on the bottom. Actually, the chosen card is face down at the bottom, and above it is the face-up card you have just shown.

Show the new top card and place it face up on the bottom in *exactly the same way*. Do the same with the next card.

When you take the fourth face-down card and turn it face-up, spectators will see the first face-up card. Everything appears normal. But you don't place the fourth card on the bottom; you leave it face up on top.

Turn the pile face down and have a spectator hold it between his hands. Clearly, you must resort to "witchcraft." Snap your fingers over the pile, and have your assistant fan the cards out, revealing the chosen card face up in the middle.

◆ The Middle Key ◆

Ask a spectator to shuffle the deck. Take the cards back and fan through them, faces towards yourself, saying, "I'm now going to memorize the entire deck. This will enable me to notice any distortion when I go through the cards again." Actually, you're going to memorize only one card. Count the cards rapidly in groups of three, noting the 26th card from the bottom. Continue through the rest of the deck.

Set the deck face down on the table. Ask your volunteer to cut the deck into three piles, approximately even. Make sure that the group from the middle of the deck is placed between the other two piles. Since it is important that onlookers realize that you cannot possibly know the card above or below the chosen card, point to the center pile, saying, "This is the group from the middle of the deck."

Ask the spectator to choose one of the outside piles. Let's assume he chooses the pile that was the original top portion of the deck. Say, "Shuffle the cards. Now look at the top card and remember it." When he is done, direct him to place the pile on top of the middle pile. He is then to take the other pile, shuffle it, and place it on top of all. The spectator may now give the deck several complete cuts.

Take the deck and run through the cards, looking for the card you noted earlier. When you find it, begin counting with the *next* card. The 26th card to the left of your key card is the one selected. If you come to the end of the deck, continue your count with the bottom card and keep counting to the left. Place the spectator's card face down on the table. He names it, and you turn it face up.

Let's go back to when the spectator chooses a pile from which to take a card. Suppose he selects the pile that was the original bottom portion of the deck. Have him shuffle it and look at the bottom card. He places the pile down, puts the middle pile on top. Then he shuffles the other pile and places it either on top or bottom. Again, he gives the deck several complete cuts. After you find your key card, you count 26 cards to the left and take out the *next* card.

In other words, if the spectator chooses a card from the top third, the card is 26 from the key card. If he chooses from the bottom third, it is 27 from the key card.

◆ No Problem At All ◆

This variation of an extremely well-known trick seems absolutely impossible.

Start by dealing a card face down on the table. Deal another to the right of it. Deal a third to the right of that card. Go back to card one and continue the deal until you have three piles of nine cards each. Ask a spectator to select a pile, look through the cards and think of one. Avert your head while he does so.

Pick up one of the other piles, place the spectator's pile on top of it, and place the third pile on top of all. Deal three piles of cards as before. Ask the spectator to look through each pile in turn and give you the pile containing his card. Again, this pile goes between the other two, forming one pile. The chosen card is now 13th, 14th, or 15th from the top.

"I'll mix these up a little," you say, and proceed to transfer 13 cards from the top to the bottom. Sloppily move the cards in groups of two, three, or four. At the end of this, the chosen card will either be on top, second from the top, or on the bottom. As you straighten the stack, tap the cards on the table so that you can see the bottom card. Then hold the pile in the dealing position in your left hand.

"What's the name of your card?" you ask. If he names the bottom card, slowly turn the stack over, showing the chosen card on the bottom. If he names another card, say, "No problem at all." Deal the top card face-up on the table. If it is the chosen card, take a bow and quit. If not, *immediately* say, "N." Transfer a card from top to bottom. Deal the next card face-up on top of the first card dealt, saying, "O. That's 'no.'" Move a card to the bottom. "Now for 'problem.'" Deal a face-up card onto the pile, saying, "P." Continue on until you have spelled "problem." In the same way, spell "at all." When you finish the spelling, do not place the next card beneath the stack. Instead, dramatically turn it face up.

RED AND BLACK

These unusual, colorful tricks are always audience-pleasers.

◆ Follow the Leader ◆

Here's a snappy trick requiring virtually no sleights and featuring two—count them, two—swindles!

Place six black cards on top of six red cards. Turn the packet face up. Hold your hands down so that all can see the faces of the cards as you spread them out. You explain, "Six red cards and six black cards." Raise your hands upwards as you close the cards up and divide them into two groups, adding a black card to the back of the reds (Illus. 33). In your left hand

Illus. 33. Divide the cards into two groups, adding a black card to the back of the reds.

are five blacks; in your right, five reds backed by a black card.

Hold the two groups separate, saying, "The reds go on top." Slide the group in your right hand behind those in the left, and turn the pile face down. On top is a black card followed by six red cards, and then five black cards.

Count off the six top cards, *one under the other*, and place them in a very neat face-down pile on the table. Say, "Six reds." Count the remaining six, one under the other, and place them in a very neat face-down pile to the left of the other pile. Say, "Six blacks."

Pick up the pile on the right and turn it face up on your left palm. Take off the bottom red card, placing it forward of the pile. "We'll need a card to mark the reds." Place the rest of the cards face down below the marker. Do precisely the same thing with the pile on the left, commenting, "And we'll also need a card to mark the blacks."

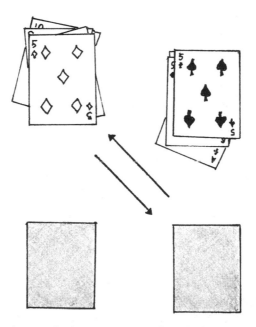

Illus. 34. Exchange the lower right card with the upper left marker; in other words, exchange diagonally.

Pause briefly. "But if we exchange markers, watch what happens."

Exchange the markers; snap your fingers. Simultaneously turn over the top face-down cards, placing them face up on their markers. "The cards follow the markers."

Exchange the markers again, snap your fingers, and once more turn the top cards over on their markers.

Swindle one: "Makes no difference how we do it," you explain. From each face-down pile, deal the top card face down on top of its marker pile. Exchange the marker piles. Snap your fingers. Turn over the card you just placed on each.

"We can exchange the piles themselves." Exchange the piles. Snap your fingers. Deal each top card on its respective marker.

Swindle two: "It just doesn't matter." Exchange the lower right card with the upper left marker pile; in other words, exchange diagonally (Illus. 34). Stall briefly: "If you could snap your fingers exactly as I do, you could do this, too." Snap your fingers. Turn each single card face up, dealing it on the pile *next to it*.

♦   Crazy Coincidence   ♦

Fan through the deck, faces towards you. Make sure no one can see what you're actually doing. Pretending to contemplate, pick out eight red cards and place them in different spots, face down on the table. Pick out eight black cards and hand them to a volunteer to shuffle briefly. Take them back and place one, face down, on each of the cards on the table.

Ask the spectator to choose a pair. Pick the two cards up and turn them over. Holding one in each hand, name them, and say, "Please remember these two cards, which were freely chosen." Name them again. Reverse the order of the two cards when you bring them together, so that the former top card is now on the bottom. Place the two on the table with the other pairs.

Have your assistant gather up the pairs, placing them into one pile. He may collect them in any order. Now he cuts the pile three times.

"Please deal the cards alternately, making two piles." When he finishes, say, "Let's see what happened to the two selected cards." Name them again. Then turn over each of the piles. In one pile, all the cards are red except for the black selected card. In the other, all are black except for the red selected card.

♦ Startling Separation ♦

Fan the cards, faces towards you. Take out a red card and place it face down on the table. Remove a black card and place it face down on top of it. Continue until you have 12 cards on the table, alternating red and black.

Ask a spectator to pick up the pile and place the cards behind his back. He is to give the packet a complete cut, and then turn over the top two cards together. He repeats this procedure as often as he wishes. Then he hands the packet back to you.

"Now it's my turn," you say, taking the packet behind your back. Deal off the top card into your right hand, turn the next card over. Continue alternating like this until you have placed all the cards into the right hand. Bring the pile forward, saying, "Six of these cards are now face up."

Deal the cards, one at a time, into two piles on the table. In one pile, deal the face up cards; in the other, the face down cards. Count the face-up cards aloud as you place them down.

"Not only did I predict the number," you say, "but also I separated the reds from the blacks." Point out that the face-up cards are all of the same color. Turn over the other pile; again the cards are all of the same color.

◆   A Matter of Choice   ◆

Toss out on the table, face up, four red cards and four black cards. Set the deck aside. Pick up a red card and place a black card on top of it. Put both cards face up in the left hand, saying, "A pair of red and black." Repeat the action three more times, each time repeating the statement. Spread the cards in a face-up fan. The colors should alternate, with a black card at the face of the group.

"Four pairs," you explain. "Each one contains a red card and a black card." Let everyone get a good look. Get a volunteer and say to him, "We are about to find out whether you have 'psychic powers' by letting you make a decision about each pair, but of course the cards will have to be face down." Turn the packet face down. "And we'll have to arrange some pairs differently so we'll know that it's a true test of your powers."

Four times you will move two cards from the top to the bottom in the following manner.

(1) Push off the top two cards with your thumb and turn them over together on top of the deck, so that all can see the faces of both cards (Illus. 35). Turn them face down together and place them, as a unit, on the bottom of the packet.

Illus. 35. Push off the top two cards with your thumb and turn them over together on top of the deck, so that all can see the faces of both cards.

(2) As with (1), push off two cards, show them, and turn them face down. Now, however, you take off the top card and push the second card off *on top of it*. Place both on the bottom of the packet. Make no attempt to be devious; you have said that you would mix the pairs.

(3) Repeat (1).

(4) Repeat (2).

At this point, from top to bottom, the packet runs R-B-B-R-R-B-B-R. "To confuse you even more, we'll start in the middle." Spread the cards face down between your hands, letting the surface of the fifth card down show more than the others (Illus. 36). Apparently, you're going to divide the cards in the

Illus. 36. Spread the cards face down between your hands, letting the surface of the fifth card down show more than the others.

middle. Actually, as you close up the fan, you take the top *five* cards in your right hand. Place the three in your left hand on top of the packet. From the top down, the packet is now arranged in alternating pairs of matching colors, the top pair being black.

Thumb off the top two cards and hold them out face down, saying, "Which one of these do you think is the black card?" Drop his choice face down onto the table and place the other card on the bottom of the packet. "Let's try another black," you say. Fan out the packet and remove as a pair the third and fourth cards from the top. He chooses one and you drop it *next to* the card on the table. Place the other card on the bottom of the packet.

"Now a red." Take the top two and offer a choice. Place the chosen card on top of the first choice, placing the other card on the bottom of the packet.

"Another red." He chooses from the top two, and you place the card on top of the second choice, the remaining card going on the bottom.

"If you have chosen correctly," you say, "each of these piles should have a black card on the bottom and a red card on top." Place one pile on top of the other. "Now the cards should alternate. From the bottom up, they should be black, red, black, red. So your next choice should be a black."

Offer him the choice of the top two. Place his selection on top of the pile on the table and place the reject on the bottom of the packet in your hand.

Have him choose a red from the next two, placing the reject below the card remaining in your hand. Take the top (black) card in your right hand and the other (red) in your left. The card in your right hand must be the next card on top of the pile on the table, so the wording is critical: "We have only two left. Which one do you want on top?" If he indicates the right hand, very deliberately place that card on top of the pile. Then turn over the other card, saying, quite pleased, "Leaving us a red." Turn the card down and place it on top of the pile.

If he indicates the left hand, place that card *on top* of the one in the right hand and place both on top of the pile, with no comment other than, "All right."

Occasionally when you ask which one he wants on top, a spectator will say, "On top of what?" Answer, "It doesn't matter Just pick either one." Then proceed as above.

Pick up the pile. "Let's see how you did." Slowly deal the cards face up and overlapping, so that all can see that your volunteer did perfectly.

◆ Double Strangers ◆

An astonishing trick, this is similar in effect to *Crazy Coincidence* on page 76, but it is much different in execution.

Get a volunteer, saying, "I need someone to assist me, someone who will be attuned to my mental vibrations."

Tell your volunteer, "I'm going to have to pick out an appropriate group of cards for us. This is very difficult." As you talk, fan through the cards so that only you can see the faces. If there is not a black card on the bottom, cut one to the bottom. Fan through the deck and find the card that matches that first black card in color and value. Slide the card over so that it joins the other on the bottom.

"This is tough. I need some very special cards." Fan through the deck; start by raising the first two black cards about 1½" above the rest. Continue by raising each red card as you come to it. Turn the cards face down. Grasp the lower cards with your right hand and the upper cards with the left. Strip out the red cards (with the two blacks on the bottom) and place them face down on the table. Set aside the rest of the cards.

"Please cut off about half of that pile," you request. Your helper does so. Pick up the remaining pile. "You have a pile, and I have a pile. Now we'll each put our pile behind our back. No peeking! We'll each mix up our cards behind our back."

The spectator will mix up his cards. You will not; instead, push off the cards from the top and smack them against the packet as though you're mixing them.

"Select one card, please. Without looking at it, place it down here on the table. I'll do the same."

The spectator brings a card forward and sets it on the table. You take one of the black cards from the bottom and set it on the table.

"You take my card and put it behind your back, and I'll take yours. Now please put that card face up in the middle of your packet. And I'll do the same."

The spectator follows your instructions. You place the spectator's card on top of your packet. Take the other black card from the bottom, turn it face up, and place it in the middle.

Bring your cards forward, saying, "Let's take a look at our packets. We'll find out if we're in tune." Fan through your face-down cards, showing the face-up black card. Have the spectator fan through his, showing the card that matches yours in color and value.

Don't let the spectator turn his cards over as you say, "That's pretty good, right? But you're probably wondering how many other matching cards there are in the two piles. Let's see what the *real* odds are against our getting a match."

Turn your cards over, showing that all the rest are red. Have the spectator do the same with his packet.

◆ One Too Many ◆

Brother John Hamman and Walt Rollins adapted a trick by Nick Trost, who worked out a variation of *that* trick. Here's my version, which eliminates any sleight of hand.

This is a "packet trick," which means a small group of prearranged cards is used. From the face of the packet, you have four face-up blacks, three face-up reds, a face-down black, a face-up black, and a face-down black. The setup is shown in Illus. 37. The black cards should be spot cards, so that spectators will tend not to notice the values.

You may simply remove the packet from your pocket face-up, making sure no one can see the other side of the group. I prefer to make it my first trick. The packet is on top when I remove the entire deck *face-up* from the card case. You can then fan through the face-up cards to the first black card in the setup, which in my case is always the three of spades. Set the rest of the deck aside.

Hold the packet in the dealing position in the left hand with the four face-up black cards on top. "Now, a little demonstration with three black cards and three red cards."

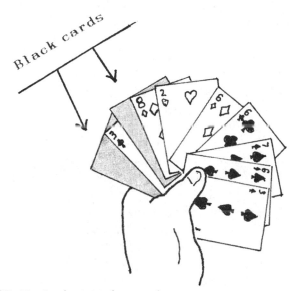

Illus. 37. Here's the initial setup for One Too Many.

Fan out the four black cards, taking them in your right hand. "Whoops! Four blacks." Toss one face up onto the table. Turn your right hand over inward (Illus. 38) and place the three blacks face down on the bottom. Square up the packet. Fan out the three red cards, calling attention to their number, and place them face down on the bottom in the same manner. Be careful not to fan too many cards, revealing the extra face-up card.

Illus. 38. Turn your right hand over inward and place the three blacks face down on the bottom.

Turn the packet over, saying, "Let's check and make sure." Fan out the three red cards, turn them over, and place them on the bottom. Fan out the four blacks, saying, "Four blacks again." Take them in your right hand and toss one onto the table. As before, place the remainder face down on the bottom.

Turn the pile over. Fan out the three blacks and place them face down on the bottom. Fan out the three reds and place them on the bottom in the usual way. "At last we're ready." Turn the packet face up. "Wait a minute! Just to be on the safe side." Pull out the bottom card, a black spot, and toss it onto the table. "*Now* let's see."

Fan the three reds and place them beneath as usual. Fan the three blacks, turn them over, *and replace them on top of the packet.* "There! It's just as well I did that." Hand the cards to a spectator, saying, "Here, you check it."

He will discover three reds and four blacks. Take the cards back. "I don't think I want to do this stunt."

◆ Miraskill Simplified ◆

Miraskill was invented by Stewart James, who created countless extraordinary tricks.

The trick is based on this: With a full deck, if you deal the cards in pairs, separating them into three piles—both red, both black, and mixed—you will end up with precisely the same number of reds and blacks. Therefore, if you remove two red cards from the deck, you will end up with two fewer reds in the red pile.

Shuffle the deck as you explain that you would like to test your power to predict the future. Turn the deck face up, saying, "Here's what I'd like you to do. Take the cards in pairs and place them in three different piles." Demonstrate by taking the first two face-up cards together and placing them in an appropriate pile. Mixed pairs go in a middle pile, black pairs to the right, and red pairs to the left. Continue dealing until you have a few red pairs and a few black pairs. Watch for a disparity of two to four cards between the black and red piles and then stop. Let us assume that there are two more cards in the black pile.

Hand the remaining cards in your hand to the spectator, telling him to give them a good shuffle. Gather up the cards on the table. Since you have two more blacks, he will have two more reds when he deals the cards out in pairs. Look through your cards and find a red two. Explain: "I am going to place a prediction card down. If it is red, it will indicate there will be that many *more* reds when you're done. If it is black, it will indicate there will be that many *more* blacks when you're done. If it's a face card, it will show that the black and red piles will be even." Place the red two to one side face down. If you can't find a red two, you can use a black two and explain: "A black card means there will be that many *fewer* black cards, and red card means that many *fewer* red cards."

Your assistant deals his cards out in pairs, counts the reds and blacks, and discovers that there are two more reds. You turn over the red two.

Add the prediction card to the cards you're still holding. Add the red pile and the black pile to the cards in your hand. Shuffle these and hand them to the spectator, asking him to shuffle further. Pick up the mixed pile and repeat your statement about the prediction card. Select a face card and set it aside face down.

When the spectator completes his deal this time, he will find that the red and black piles are equal, and your prediction is correct.

♦ Cross Hands ♦

Remove from the deck 12 red cards and 12 black cards. Call no attention to the number. Hold the red pile face up in your right hand, the black pile face up in your left hand. Deal one card from each group simultaneously, beginning two piles. Simply thumb off the top face-up card and let it drop as you withdraw your hand. On your left is a black card, and on your right a red one. Cross your hands and drop a red card on the black one, and a black card on the red one (Illus. 39). Return the hands to their original position, dealing a black card on the red one, and a red card on the black one. Continue back and forth until all the cards are dealt.

Illus. 39. Cross your hands and drop a red card on the black one, and a black card on the red one.

Point out that the cards are alternately red and black. Place one pile on top of the other and turn the entire packet face down. You will now deal the cards from the top of the packet into two piles, like this: Deal the first card face up. To its right deal the second card face up. Deal the third card face up on the first card, but overlap it downward an inch or two so that the value of both cards can be seen. Deal the fourth card face up on the card on your right, overlapping it downward. Continue dealing the cards alternately into two piles.

Name the colors as you deal the cards face up, like this: "Red, black, red, black, etc." After you have dealt 12 cards face up (six in each pile), *start dealing face down.* Continue overlapping and continue saying, "Red, black, red, black." Do not stop, or change the rhythm of the deal.

When you're done dealing, very deliberately take the two face-down piles of six cards and exchange them. "We put some blacks with the reds and some reds with the blacks," you say. "But with a snap of the fingers . . . " Snap. " . . . we find that birds of a feather flock together."

Turn the face-down cards over, showing that they now match in color the others in their respective piles.

The trick can be repeated a few times with little chance of detection.

If a spectator thinks he can do it, give him an *odd number* of black cards and the same number of reds. He will fail. The trick only works with an even number of reds and blacks.

♦ Alternate Choice ♦

I recently developed this idea for setting up the cards right before the eyes of the audience.

The point is that you don't exactly *make* a setup; instead, you get rid of all the cards that interfere with your setup. Fan through the cards, faces towards you. Say, "There are a number of nasty cards which cause 'psychic static' and disrupt the 'magical flow.' So I'm going to get rid of those cards." You want to be left with cards that alternate red and black. So as you fan through, toss out face up all the cards that break this sequence. Suppose the bottom card is black, the next three cards are red, and the next one is black. Pass the black card and the first red card to your right hand. Toss out the next two cards—reds—face up. Continue tossing out all the cards that break the sequence. I separate the offending cards in my left hand and, with the aid of the left thumb, drop them onto the table, but any method will do.

When you get rid of the last of the nasty cards, make sure that the top and bottom cards of your packet are of different colors. This means that no matter how much the stack is cut, the alternate order will persist.

Push the nasty cards aside and give your stack several quick cuts, simulating an overhand shuffle. Set the packet down and invite a volunteer to give it some complete cuts. Turn away and say, "Please give the cards one complete cut. Then take off the two top cards and look them over. Toss one aside. Remember the other one and stick it in the middle of the pile somewhere."

Turn back, inviting the spectator to give the packet more complete cuts if he wishes. Pick up the packet and fan through, faces towards you, until you find two cards of the same color next to each other. Cut between these, bringing one to the bottom and the other to the top. Note the name of the one that goes to the bottom. Ask the spectator the name of his card. Reveal his card by either turning over the top card or turning the deck over.

Discard the chosen card, and you'll be ready to repeat the trick.

◆ Mixed Colors ◆

Ask a volunteer to remove seven black cards and seven red cards from the deck. You explain that seven is a mystical number. Actually, any number will work. When you take the cards, casually shuffle them, explaining, "I am about to set up the cards to predict the exact choices you will make." The shuffling prevents spectators from perceiving the nature of your setup.

Don't let anyone see the faces of the cards as you fan through and move whatever cards are necessary to separate the reds and blacks. It makes no difference whether blacks or reds are on top.

Hold the cards in your left hand as you explain: "You will choose seven cards, and I will take the rest. We'll go through one card at a time. If you want a card, say, 'Yes.' You may take no card or several cards in a row—whatever you wish. Do you

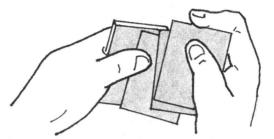

Illus. 40. You take yours one under the other. Add the rejected card to the bottom of those in your right hand.

want the top card?" Suppose he says yes. Extend the packet towards him, telling him to take the card and start a pile in front of him. If he says no, you take the card in your right hand. Continue to the end of the pile, counting aloud each time he takes a card.

The spectator places his cards in a pile, and—this is vital!—you take yours *one under the other.* You do this in a perfectly natural manner, adding the rejected card to the bottom of those in your right hand (Illus. 40).

After the spectator has seven cards, add the remainder (if any) to the bottom of the stack in your right hand. Place the two piles side by side. "Every single pair," you announce, "will consist of a black card and a red card." Turn over the top card of each pile, placing the card in front of its pile. Continue through the rest of the cards.

♦ **The World Revisited** ♦

The final offering in this section is a version of Paul Curry's *Out of This World.*

You need a packet of ten black cards and ten red cards. On top should be one black card, followed by ten red cards, and then nine black cards. The spectators should be unaware of this arrangement. At the end, I will explain a method of accomplishing this.

Hand the packet to a spectator and ask him to turn over the top card. "Good, a black card." Make it a point to name the card, as, "Oh, the six of spades. Would you please place the six of spades face up on the bottom." After he does this, ask, "What's the next card?" He turns it up. "A red card. Would you place that face up on the table? Now if you think the next card is red, place it face down on the red card on the table. If you think it's black, place it face down on the bottom." He is to continue to do this.

After he has made a choice of *eight* cards, stop him, saying, "That's enough. I think you're starting to weaken. Turn over the next card. Ah, it's red. Please place that face up on the bottom." After he does that, say, "What's the next card? A black card. Place that face up on the table next to the other cards." When he is ready, say, "Now if you think the next card is black, place it face down on the black card on the table. If you think it's red, place it face down on the bottom of the deck."

Have him continue to do this until he arrives at the face-up black card—in our example, the six of spades. Take the packet from the spectator and lift off the black card. Gesture with it as you say, "The six of spades. Back to where we started." You are holding the card face up; keep it face up as you casually place it on the bottom of the packet.

To build suspense and to distract the spectators, spend a moment complimenting the spectator on his work. You might say, "I don't know if you got any right, but you seemed very confident. I like that." Babble on a bit. Then fan through the cards in your hand to the face-up red card. Lift off the red card along with all the cards above it. Set the pile on the table, letting the face-up red card show at the bottom. Do the same with the remaining cards, letting the black card show at the bottom.

All that remains is to show each of the packets. Your volunteer has separated the cards perfectly!

Now let's get back to that original arrangement. Start fanning through the deck, faces towards you. "I need reds and blacks," you say, dropping on the table face up a mixed pair, the black card uppermost. Turn the pair face down. You now add, face down, four pairs of red cards, murmuring, "Red and black," as you drop each pair. Remove another mixed pair and drop them face up on the pile, the red card uppermost. Shake your head at your stupidity as you notice what you have done. Turn the pair down on top of the pile. Now add, face down, four pairs of black cards.

Even up the pile. Give the packet several quick complete cuts, as though shuffling overhand. Set the packet down and ask the spectator to give it a few complete cuts. Pick up the packet and fan through faces towards you, murmuring, "They seem to be pretty well mixed." Cut the cards so that a single black card is on top, followed by ten reds, and then nine blacks. Hand the packet face down to the spectator and proceed.

PLAYFUL POKER

After performing card tricks, you will often be asked if you could cheat at cards. Perform a few clever poker tricks, and let the questioner draw his own conclusion.

◆ Face-Up Draw Poker ◆

You must have a complete deck of 52 cards, and you must have the aces on the bottom. If you did a four-ace trick earlier, you can fan through and cut them to the bottom, or you can fan through, placing insignificant cards on top and the aces on the bottom, explaining that you need to stack the cards.

You can riffle-shuffle, leaving the bottom four cards. Or you can do a *Hindu Shuffle* (see page 7), pulling the first group from the middle, or both.

"How about a game of showdown?" you say. Deal four hands face-up; the first three are to different spectators, and the last hand is yours. Examine all the hands, feigning disappointment. As you gather up the cards and place them on the bottom, say, "I didn't do a very good job. Let's make it showdown, except you can draw as many cards as you want."

Again deal four face-up hands. Help the three spectators decide how many cards to discard. Just make sure that the total number is seven or eight. Deal the drawn cards *face down* to each spectator. Regardless of the quality of your hand, express dissatisfaction with it. Draw five cards face down.

Have the spectators turn their cards face up. "I have no idea of what I got," you say. "I probably lose."

But you don't; you hold the four aces.

◆ Aces Beat Kings ◆

Arrange to have the four kings on top with the four aces beneath. You can false-shuffle the cards, leaving the eight cards in that position. Hand the deck to a volunteer. Ask him to deal two piles, alternating, as though he is dealing a two-handed card game. After he has dealt twenty cards or so, say, "Stop whenever you wish."

When he stops, take the rest of the cards from him and set them aside. Ask him to pick up one of the piles and deal it into two piles. Then ask him to pick up the other pile and deal it into two piles.

"Let's see how you did," you say. Turn over and set aside the top card of each pile. All kings.

"Now let's see how *I* did." Turn over the new top card of each pile. All aces.

♦ Crooked Flush ♦

You may decide to do this for your first trick. As you remove the deck from its case, you explain. "I have stacked the deck just to demonstrate how slick gamblers can be." On top of the deck you have, from top to bottom, this setup: 4D—JD—2D—JC—AD—9C—3D—7C—5D—JH—10C—8C. You may give the cards a false cut or a *False Hindu Shuffle* (see page 9), retaining the stack on top.

"Card sharks are clever," you explain. "They often try to trap the unsuspecting." Casually deal two hands, one to a spectator and one to yourself.

"Since I stacked the cards, I know you have a pretty good hand. But without even looking, I know I have a *superb* hand." Turn your head away and show your hand. You have three jacks, and he has a small straight flush.

Move your bottom card to the top of your packet. Pick up the deck and say, "Cards?" Your volunteer should stand pat, but if he decides to draw cards, take them from the bottom, saying, "Because I'm a sneak, you get yours from the bottom."

Discard the top two from your hand, and deal yourself two. The natural assumption is that you have kept your three jacks. "If this were a real game, would you be willing to bet?" It doesn't matter. "What have you got?" He still has a small straight flush. "You have an excellent hand." Show your *high* straight flush. "But you can never be too careful."

♦ A Royal Coincidence ♦

You need the assistance of two spectators. Say, "Free of charge. I am going to give out royal flushes. Ace, king, queen, jack, and ten of the same suit." Ask the first spectator which suit he wants. Fan through the cards face up and find the jack of the selected suit. Place this face up in front of the spectator. Then, in any order, find the other cards and place them, one at a time, on top of the pile you started with the jack.

Ask spectator two which suit he wants. This time, the jack must be the third card in the pile, so place two of the others face up before adding the jack. Then complete the flush. Turn each of the piles face down. Spectator one has the jack on top, and spectator two has the jack third from the top.

"I believe I'll take one for myself," you say, and remove another royal flush from the deck in the same way as you did the others. The jack must be the second card placed face up. Pick up your flush, saying, "I want you each to choose a card from your flush. Here's the way you'll do it."

Holding the cards face up, place one card under the pile and deal the next to the table. Place one under, and deal the next on top of the card on the table. Continue until you hold only one card. Drop it on the pile. "This would be the selected card," you say. "Of course, the deal is done face down." Pick up the pile and turn it face down. Repeat the deal. Lift up the last card and show it.

"All sorts of possibilities," you say. With the cards face down, repeat the deal once more, again showing the last card. You have now shown three different cards resulting from the elimination process; the fact that one of the deals was face up seems irrelevant. "You may do as many deals as you wish. But before you begin, I have to do something strange with my cards."

Place your cards behind your back. Turn the second card from the top, the jack, face up. Move the bottom card to the top. The jack is now face up in the middle of your pile. Bring the pile forward and set it on the table.

Address the first spectator: "To make sure the deals are different, I would like you to do the complete deal any *even* number of times . . . " Address spectator two: " . . . and you any *odd* number of times."

So that you can provide guidance, have the first spectator do his eliminations, and then the second spectator. In each instance, make sure the top card is not turned up.

Spread out your pile, showing the jack face up in the middle. Have the spectators turn over their top cards, which are also jacks.

FOUR-ACE TRICKS

People just love tricks with four aces. The proficient card handler should be able to present one or two really good ones.

◆ Spelling the Aces ◆

With a bit of memory work, you can perform a feat which simply *has* to be either magic or superb sleight of hand, but it's just subtlety. I developed a method of spelling the aces, using an adaptation of Gene Finell's "Free-Cut Principle."

You will need a full 52-card deck. Remove from the deck the four aces and the queen of spades, tossing them on the table face up. "The queen of spades is supposed to have magical properties," you say. "Let's see if she can accomplish anything with the four aces."

Holding the deck face down, rapidly fan through the cards in groups of three until you have nine cards. Even them up and place the group face down on the table to your left. Fan off ten cards the same way and place them to the right of the first pile. Do the same with another group of ten cards. Place the remaining cards to the right of all. "Whoops! I'll need another pile. Just a few cards will do." Take two cards from the top of your last pile and place these as a separate pile to the left of your first pile.

As you look at them, the piles are set up like this:

2   9   10   10   16

Place the ace of clubs face up on the second pile from the left. Place the ace of hearts face up on the pile to the right

Illus. 41. The layout of the aces and the queen of spades.

of it. Place the queen of spades face up on the pile to the right of that. Place the ace of spades face up on top of the farthest pile to the right. And place the ace of diamonds to the right of that pile (Illus. 41). The aces go down in this order: clubs, hearts, spades, diamonds (CHaseD), and the queen of spades goes in the middle of the aces.

Say to a spectator, "Please turn the ace of clubs face down and place it on this pile." Indicate the two-card pile. "Now cut off some cards from this pile . . . " Indicate the pile from which the ace of clubs came. " . . . and place them on top of the ace of clubs."

Point to the ace of hearts. "Now turn this one face down and place it on top of this pile." Indicate the pile to your left of the pile on which the ace of hearts rests. "And cut off some cards from that pile . . . " Point to the pile from which the ace of hearts came. " . . . and place them on the ace of hearts."

In the same way, have him move the queen of spades to the next pile to your left. "But the queen of spades has work to do," you explain, "so let's keep her face up." Again cards are cut from the pile on which the queen of spades had rested and are placed on top of the queen of spades.

The ace of spades is treated the same way, except that it's turned face down. Pick up the ace of diamonds, turn it face down, and place it on top of the pile on your far right, saying, "And I'll take care of the ace of diamonds myself."

Gather the cards from right to left, placing the pile on your far right on the pile next to it, placing both on the next pile, and so on.

"Three is a mystic number," you say, "so would you please cut the cards three times. This will give the queen of spades a chance to go through the deck and work her magic." After the cuts, pick up the cards and, holding them face down, fan through to the queen of spades. Set the pile which is *above* the queen onto the table. Take the queen in your right hand. "The question is, 'Did the queen do her work?' We'll soon find out."

Toss the queen aside. Transfer the cards from your left hand to your right and drop them onto the pile on the table. Draw the deck towards you, picking it up. "Now let's see if we can spell out the aces. Here's what we'll do. We'll spell out an ace, dealing a card for each letter, and the ace should come out on the last letter. For instance, let's try the ace of hearts."

Spell *ace of hearts*, dealing one card into a face-down pile for each letter in the spelling. Turn the last card in the spelling face up. Let everyone see that it is the ace of hearts, then toss it aside face up with the queen of spades. Leave the dealt pile on the table.

Spectators will now choose the order in which the remaining aces are spelled. "What's another good ace?" you ask.

Whenever the ace of spades is named, you turn the deck face up and spell *ace of spades*, making a separate pile. Toss the ace of spades aside with the other ace(s) and queen of spades. Turn the dealt cards face down on the table. Turn over the cards in your hand so that they're back in the face-down dealing position.

You have only two aces to worry about—diamonds and clubs.

If diamonds is called before clubs:

Spell *ace of diamonds* from the top of the deck and toss it aside with the others. If the ace of spades has already been spelled, place all other piles, including the cards in your hand, on top of the pile just dealt. Turn the deck face up and spell *ace of clubs*.

If the ace of spades has *not* already been spelled, set the deck down to the left of the pile just dealt. Place the pile you used to spell the ace of hearts on top of the pile just dealt. You now have two piles on the table. When the ace of spades is called, you pick up the pile on the left, turn it face up and spell it. When the ace of clubs is called, you pick up the pile on the right, turn it face up and spell it.

If clubs is called before diamonds:

Spell *ace of clubs* from the top of the deck and toss it aside with the others. The ace of diamonds is now the third card from the top of the deck.

If the ace of spades has already been spelled, drop the deck on top of the pile you just made spelling the ace of clubs. Place the deck on top of one of the two other piles. Pick up the last pile and place it on top. You are now in position to spell *ace of diamonds* from the top.

If the ace of spades has not yet been spelled, set the remainder of the deck (the cards in your hand) to the left of the other piles. Say, "We'd better put the deck together." Point to the pile you just set down, saying to a spectator, "Please cut several cards from the top of this pile." This statement ensures that he will cut off at least three cards and that he won't cut past the ace of spades.

Pick up the pile you just made spelling the ace of clubs and place it on top of the remainder of the deck. On top of this, the spectator places the cards he just cut off. On top of all, place the other pile (the one you used to spell the ace of hearts). You are now in position to spell *ace of diamonds* from the face-down deck or *ace of spades* from the face-up deck.

Apparently the aces are lost in the deck, yet you're able to spell them out *as called for*. It seems impossible. Yet mastery of this trick should take you no more than an hour or so of practice.

♦ The Wandering Ace ♦

Very openly collect the four aces at the bottom of the deck.

With the deck face up, fan out the four aces and lift them off, displaying them. As you do so, with your left thumb, push off the next face card on the deck very slightly. Draw it back, obtaining a little-finger break beneath it. Close up the fan of aces against the base of your left thumb, letting the right fingers slide under the fifth card, adding it to your stack. Flip the rest of the deck over with your left thumb. Turn the five cards face down and casually toss them on top of the deck.

Fan out the top four cards, take them off the deck, even them up, and place them face down on the table.

Have a card selected and turned face up so all can see it. Take the card and place it face down on top of the deck. Cut the deck. Set the deck down.

"Now let's put the four aces to work." Pick up the four cards on the table and deal them one at a time on top of the deck. Tap the deck. Deal off three aces one at a time face up. Turn over the next card; look puzzled. "Where is the other ace?"

Spread the cards face up, showing that the ace has penetrated right through half the deck to join the chosen card.

♦ An Ace Surprise ♦

Spectators assist as all four aces are magically cut.

This is a variation of a famous force, to which I have added a few wrinkles. You need to have four aces on top of the deck. Suppose that you have performed a four-ace trick several tricks before. Chances are the aces are together somewhere in the deck. Simply fan through and cut them to the top.

"We'll select four cards," you explain. "I'll choose the first one and show you how we're going to do it."

Hold the deck in your left hand in the dealing position. With your left thumb push off fifteen or twenty cards, taking them at the center of the right edge in the right hand. Turn this group face up onto the deck.

On each succeeding cut, you will begin fanning the cards

below the face-up cards. The reason for this is that you don't wish to expose the faces of the aces.

Fan through at least fifteen of the face-down cards. Separate the cards at that point. In your right hand are fifteen to twenty face-up cards and below them are some fifteen face-down cards. Turn the entire stack over and replace it on top of the deck. Fan down through the face-up cards to the first face-down card. Separate the cards at this point, taking the first face-down card (an ace) with the tips of the right fingers and holding it at the bottom of the stack in your right hand (Illus. 42). Drop this card face down on the table. Address a volunteer:

Illus. 42. Take the first face-down card (an ace) with the tips of the right fingers and hold it at the bottom of the stack in your right hand.

"And you will need an indicator card." With the tips of your right fingers, push off the bottom face-up card of those in your right hand and either drop it face up on the table or hand it to your volunteer.

"We'll use your card to mark where you want the cards cut." As with the previous cut, fan through the first ten to fifteen face-down cards, and then spread several out, saying, "Stick your card in face up, so I'll know where to cut. But hang on to the card; we'll need to use it again."

Separate the cards at the point at which he inserts the face-up card, taking the cards above the break in your right hand

and turning them over onto the deck. Again he inserts the face-up card among the face-down cards, and again you separate the cards at that point and turn the packet over onto the deck. As before, fan down through the face-up cards to the first face-down card. Lift off the face-up cards with the right hand, again taking with them the first face-down card (an ace). Drop the ace face down on the table next to the first ace.

Let your helper hang on to his indicator card as you approach a second spectator. Again push off the bottom face-up card of those in your right hand and give it to your volunteer. "You will also need a card to mark where you want the cards cut." This procedure is necessary; otherwise, spectators will see the same face-up card each time an ace is cut.

The second spectator inserts the indicator card twice for the cuts, and another ace is dropped onto the table next to the other two. The procedure is repeated with a third spectator.

At the conclusion, you turn all the cards in the deck face down and set the deck aside. Gather the indicator cards and place them on top of the deck. "We have chosen four cards, and to be perfectly dishonest with you, I have no idea of what they are. Let's take a look." Turn the four cards face up, revealing the aces.

◆ Aces Up ◆

Similar in execution to *Double Strangers* (see page 81), the effect is quite different. You must have the four aces at the bottom of the deck. You can give the cards a *Hindu Shuffle* (see page 7), pulling the first packet from the middle.

Ask a volunteer to cut off about half the deck and place the cards behind his back. You place the rest behind your back. He is to pick out a card from anywhere in his packet and hand it to you face down; you are to hand him a card from your packet face down. The one you give him is an ace from the bottom of your group. Behind his back, the spectator is to turn the card over and stick it somewhere in his packet. You are to do the same. Actually, place the card he hands you on top, turn over an ace from the bottom and stick it in the middle.

The two of you repeat the procedure. Then both of you bring your cards forward. "Let's see what we chose." Fan through both piles. Two aces are face up in each pile.

SILLY STUFF

You greatly enhance the entertainment value of a routine of card tricks when you occasionally throw in amusing or nonsensical stunts. Here are some of the best.

◆ Great Expectorations ◆

Fan through a deck of cards and toss on the table face up all the cards of one suit. Arrange them so that, from top to bottom, they run from Ace down to the 2: A-K-Q-J-10-9-8-7-6-5-4-3-2. Show the arrangement to one and all.

Turn the pile face down and say, "I'm going to deal the cards face down on the table. Whenever you want me to double-dip, holler, 'Spit.' "

Deal the cards slowly into a face-down pile. When someone shouts "Spit," take the card you're holding and push off the next card in the deck, taking it *on top* of the one in your hand. Drop the two cards together on top of the pile. As you take the two cards and drop them, say, "Okay, let's do a double-dip." Do the same when anyone shouts, "Spit."

Pick up the pile and repeat the deal, "spitting" when told to do so. "The cards should be sufficiently mixed." Turn over the pile; the cards are in precisely the same order as they were at the beginning.

You can repeat, going through the cards *four* times. In fact, any even number of times will work. The double-dip, of course, doesn't change the relative order of the cards at all.

If you want everyone to have the fun of catching on, you might repeat the stunt several times.

♦ In My Pocket ♦

"Are you ready for real magic?" you ask. "I want anyone here to name a card, and I will instantly remove that card from my pocket."

Someone names a card; you reach into your pocket and remove a deck of cards. "It's right here, ladies and gentlemen." Thumb through the cards until you come to the chosen one, remove it, and hold it up, proudly announcing its name.

♦ The Dancing King ♦

Steve Martin performed this stunt for Johnny Carson on the "Tonight Show."

Remove a king from the deck and hold it up so all can see it. "I would like to perform for you now the famous *Dancing King Trick.*"

Hold the king so that it rests on its edge on a table or chair, the face towards spectators (Illus. 43). "When I count to three,

Illus. 43. Hold the king so that it rests on its edge on a table or chair, the face towards spectators.

I would like you all to say, 'Dance, king, dance.' Ready?"

Count to three; the group says, "Dance, king, dance." Rapidly bounce the king around, on one edge and then the other, moving it up an inch or so with each movement, as you make the king dance.

◆ The Cutting Edge ◆

When you have a chance to do so unobserved, turn the bottom card of the deck face up and then turn the entire deck over. You have one card face down on top while all the others are face up.

Approach a spectator, saying, "Please cut off a pile of cards, and I will *instantly* name the card you cut to."

The pile is cut off; you see the face-up card and name it. After taking the cards back from the spectator, restore the deck to its proper order. Some will think you have actually performed a trick; most will think you're just silly.

◆ Eventually ◆

Have a card selected. Sight the bottom card and undercut the deck for replacement. In this way you learn the card above the chosen card. Immediately start dealing the cards from the face-down deck into a face-up pile. Deal until you come to the card you sighted. Stop and say, "Is this your card?" No.

Turn the deck face up and deal several cards face up into the same pile. Stop and indicate the last card you dealt. Ask if it is the chosen card. Again, no. Note the card facing you on the bottom of the deck. Turn the remaining cards face down and give the cards one cut at about the middle.

Again deal the cards face up from the face-down deck until you come to the card you just noted on the bottom. Repeat the questioning process. Turn the deck face up again and deal off several cards as before. Ask the spectator if you've found his card. No such luck. Turn the deck face down, feigning complete bewilderment.

You should now be holding no more than ten cards. Casually shuffle the top (chosen) card to the bottom. Deal the cards face up from the packet until the only card remaining in your hand is the one chosen. Ask if the last face-up card dealt is the spectator's card. He says no, of course.

Ask the name of the selected card. Turn over the last card. Say, "I knew I'd find it eventually."

◆ A Card Adherent ◆

A chosen card is returned and brought to the bottom of the deck. "We'll need to have these mixed." Hand the top third to a spectator, saying, "You shuffle half." Hand another third to another spectator, saying, "You shuffle half." Turn away with the rest. "And I'll turn away and shuffle half." Comment: "It's a big deck."

Shuffle the chosen card to the top. Moisten your thumb and press it near the top center of the chosen card. Turn around and take the two piles from the spectators in your left hand

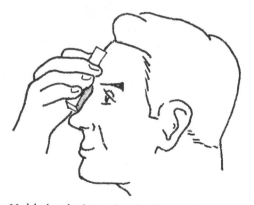

Illus. 44. Hold the deck in the dealing position in your right hand and press the back of the deck firmly against your forehead.

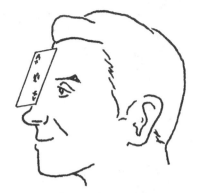

Illus. 45. The chosen card remains stuck to your forehead.

and place them below your pile. Hold the deck in the dealing position in your *right* hand and press the back of the deck firmly against your forehead (Illus. 44). "I'm concentrating on your card, trying to pick up the name. No, it's just no use."

Move your right hand down in a firm sweeping motion, removing the deck from your face. The chosen card remains stuck to your forehead (Illus. 45). "I'm sorry I just can't get it. Nothing sticks in my mind. In fact, I'm starting to see spots before my eyes."

After you play it for all it's worth, you suddenly discover the card on your forehead.

◆ The Invisible Deck—1 ◆

Many years ago, I created this amusing stunt to disguise an antique card trick.

Say, "You've seen me try a number of experiments with this deck, but I'd like to try one with my other deck."

Set the deck aside, reach into your pocket, and remove an imaginary deck. It is vital that you treat the invisible deck *exactly* as you would a regular deck. Shuffle the imaginary deck, saying, "Some people can see the deck, and some people can't." Pick out a fun-loving spectator and say to him, "You look as though you can see the cards, sir. Is that correct?" It usually is correct.

Fan the invisible deck in front of him, asking him to think of one of the cards he sees. "Do you have one? Fine." Set the invisible deck down and ask him to cut it. Whatever he does, say, "Quit the clowning. The cards are right here." Give the invisible deck a cut.

"Now I'm going to find your ... Just a minute! Some of the others can't see the deck." Fan the real deck in front of your helper and have him pick out his card and show it to the other spectators. When he returns it, bring it to the top of the deck. Give the cards a false shuffle, retaining the top card.

"Now give me a number from, say, five to twenty ... and your card will appear at that number." He gives you a number. Count the cards into a pile and turn over the card at his number. "And here's your ... No, wait a minute! That's not your card; I forgot something."

Turn the card face down. As you say the following, even the cards by tapping them on the table lengthwise, glancing at the bottom, chosen, card. "We're supposed to use the invisible deck first."

Return the packet to the top of the deck, putting his card at the selected number. Pick up the invisible deck and count down to the spectator's number, turning over the last, invisible, card.

"And there it is ... " Name the selected card. Turn the invisible card face down on the invisible pile, and place the pile on top of the rest of the invisible deck. Set the invisible deck aside.

"Now we can check the visible deck." Count down in the real deck, and, sure enough, his card is there.

Be sure to pick up the invisible deck, give it a last shuffle, and place it in your pocket.

♦   The Invisible Deck—2   ♦

Before putting the invisible deck away, you may want to try another trick. Again fan the invisible cards for a spectator to note one and remember it.

"Let's make this really confusing," you say. "Multiply the value of your card by ten. Add eight. If your card is a club, add one. Add two for a heart, three for a spade, and four for a diamond." (You can remember the order by thinking of the word CHaseD.)

Ask the spectator for the total. You subtract eight. The first digit gives you the value, the second gives you the suit. For example, the spectator tells you 100. You subtract eight, giving you 92. The card is the nine of hearts. (Remember? Two for a heart.)

Look through the invisible deck, find his card and hand it to him, naming it.

♦   Let Me Spell It Out   ♦

Saying that you want to make sure there's no joker in the deck, fan through the cards and cut the ten of spades to the top. Ask a spectator to cut off a small packet of cards and turn them face up on the deck. Then ask him to cut off a larger portion and turn them over on the deck. Fan through the face-up cards to the first face-down card. Have the spectator look at it, show it around, and stick it somewhere in the middle of the face-down cards. He has chosen the ten of spades. Turn the face-up cards face down, and have the spectator give the entire deck a thorough shuffle.

As you take the deck back, say, "Let me spell it out for you. I'm first going to reveal the suit . . . and then the value." You are about to remove nine cards from the deck; none of them should be spades. First place any six face up on the table, saying, "Six." Take out a picture card and place it face up on the six, saying, "Picture card." Remove an ace and add it to the pile, saying, "Ace." Remove a two and add it to the pile, saying, "Deuce." In the same way, remove an eight and then a seven.

"Do these in any way remind you of the suit of your card?" They don't. Turn the pile face down. "Don't worry, I'll have a lucky spell in a minute."

Remove a three and start a new pile, saying, "Three." In the same way add an eight and a nine. "Do these bring to mind the value?" No. Turn the three-card pile face down. "What *is* your card?" The ten of spades.

"Look, let me spell it out for you." Pick up the first pile you laid out. "The suit is spades." Deal out each card face up as you explain. "S as in six, P as in picture card, A as in ace, D as in deuce, E as in eight, S as in seven, S-P-A-D-E-S, spades." Pick up the three-card pile and turn over the cards as you explain: "The value is ten. T as in three, E as in eight, N as in nine, T-E-N, ten. The ten of spades. Hey, were you trying to kid me?"

◆ Hair Pull ◆

A card is chosen and brought to the top of the deck. Hold the deck in your left hand, parallel to the length of your hand. Note that your fingers grip the end so that the cards are pushed against the base of your thumb. This makes it easier to perform the necessary action with your left thumb (Illus. 46).

Pretend to pull a long hair from your head with your right hand. Pantomime tying an end of it to the upper right corner of the deck. "Let's see if I can pull your card out of the deck."

Grasp the loose end of your invisible hair and pull it up and over. As you do so, swing the top card up with your left thumb (Illus. 47). If the timing is right, the effect is quite surprising ... and amusing.

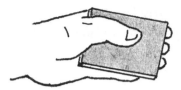

Illus. 46. Note that your fingers grip the end so that the cards are pushed against the base of your thumb. This makes it easier to perform the necessary action with your left thumb.

Illus. 47. (right) Grasp the loose end of your invisible hair and pull it up and over. As you do so, swing the top card up with your left thumb.

◆ And So Fourth ◆

Fan through the deck, ostensibly to make sure the joker isn't there. Actually, note the fourth card from the top. False shuffle or false cut, leaving the card in position.

Suppose the fourth card were the six of spades. "Now . . . a stupendous feat of magic! Six of spades, come forth!" Turn over the top card. Not there. Check the bottom card. Not there either. Try again: "Six of spades, come forth!" Again it is not on the top or bottom.

"Six of spades, come forth!" you repeat. "Wait a minute. I think the cards *are* obeying me." Deal off cards from the top, saying, "First, second, third, fourth." Show the six of spades.

You may prefer this variation: Have a card chosen and bring it fourth from the top. Locate it, as above.

♦ As Time Goes By ♦

You want the chosen card second from the top. When the spectator replaces his card, you can secure a little-finger break one card above it and then perform the *Triple-Cut Control* (page 10). Another good method is described in *Upsy-Daisy*, page 69.

Ask, "How many weeks in a year?" Fifty-two is the response. Count off five cards into a pile, and two cards into another pile. Put the "two pile" on top of the "five pile" and replace the cards on top of the deck.

"How many months in a year?" Count off 12 cards and replace them on top. "How many days in a week?" Count off seven cards and replace them on top.

"What time is it?" Whatever the answer, say, "Wrong! It's time to find your card. What is your card?" Turn over the top one.

♦ The Nose Knows ♦

While toying with the deck, peek at the bottom card. Casually shuffle it to the top.

"Ladies and gentlemen," you announce, "with this ordinary pack of 52 cards, I am about to perform a miracle." Concentrate and then name the card you peeked at. "Yes, I am fully capable of naming a card. But now comes the hard part."

Directly face the group, holding the deck in your left hand. Grasping it at the sides between the tip of your thumb and fingertips, place it directly in front of your face (Illus. 48). The audience should be able to see the bottom card. Press the bottom portion of the deck against your nose.

Slowly raise your head as you gradually lower the deck. The card you announced rises from the back of the deck (Illus. 49). After the card has risen a little more than half its length, take it away with the other hand. Lower the deck from your face,

Illus. 48. Hold the deck in your left hand. Grasping it at the sides between the tip of your thumb and fingertips, place it directly in front of your face.

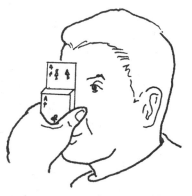

Illus. 49. Slowly raise your head as you gradually lower the deck. The card you announced rises from the back of the deck.

muttering, "If you want to be a great magician, you have to learn to use your head."

◆ Evil Spell ◆

For this stunt you need ten cards. From top to bottom, these are the cards: 3-5-A-7-9-2-queen of spades-8-6-4. Except for the queen of spades, the suits are irrelevant. No reason not to make the setup in plain sight.

Spell the word "ace," transferring one card to the bottom for the "a" and another to the bottom for the "c." On "e" turn over the third card from the top, the ace, and toss it face up on the table. Spell out two and three the same way, tossing each into the pile begun with the ace.

Ask a volunteer to spell out four. When he turns over the last card, it is the queen of spades. "No, no," you say. "The queen of spades is bad luck. Here's the way you do it." Make sure the queen is returned to the top. Spell out four, tossing it on the table with the others. The spectator tries spelling five and gets the queen of spades, which is returned to the top. You spell five and toss the card on the table.

The spectator spells six and gets the queen of spades. "I keep telling you that's bad luck," you say, taking the cards back. You properly spell out the six. And then the seven.

The spectator fails with the eight, but you don't. The same with the nine. You are left with the queen of spades. Turn it over saying, "I know you really like the queen of spades. I'd give you permanent possession, but it would ruin the deck."

The spectator gets the queen of spades on the following deals: four, five, six, eight, and nine.

♦ **Number Nonsense** ♦

This droll idea came to me one night just as I was dropping off to sleep. How I wish all my ideas came as easily! As you will perhaps recognize, the stunt is based on an old vaudeville routine.

Debbi seems willing to assist, so have her shuffle the deck and then deal the entire deck into five hands. When she finishes, have her select one of the hands, shuffle it, look at the top card, and show it around (but not to you). She then replaces the card on top and sets the pile down.

The last three hands that were dealt contain ten cards each. Two of these must go on top of Debbi's pile. Invite a second spectator to pick up one of these two piles, shuffle it, and place some of its cards on top of Debbi's pile. Point to another of the ten-card piles and ask a third spectator to pick it up, shuffle it, and place some of its cards on top of Debbi's pile. The second spectator is told to put the rest of his cards on top of the pile. And the third spectator is told the same.

Pick up the pile and add the remaining two hands to the bottom. The chosen card is now 21st from the top.

You may choose to bring the selected card to the 21st position using the method given in *Gentle Persuasion*, page 52.

Address Debbi: "I'm about to bring your chosen card to a number you name. Give me any number between 20 and 30." This limits her choices to nine numbers. You further limit the choice if she should say 21, for you immediately say, "Except 21."

When she gives the number, repeat it a few times so that all will remember. Suppose she chooses the number 28.

Now for the fun! Deliberately deal three cards into a pile, saying, "One, two, three," as you do. Stop, looking puzzled. "I always have trouble remembering certain numbers. What's supposed to be the unlucky number?" Someone will respond 13. "13," you repeat, and then continue dealing. "14, 15, 16." Stop again.

"Does anyone remember how many lives a cat is supposed to have?" Someone says 9. You repeat the number and continue dealing: "10, 11, 12." Once more you're perplexed.

"If 13 is bad luck, which number is good luck?" Someone says 7. Now you actually get tricky. You mentally subtract from 40 the number the spectator originally selected. This gives you the next number you will stop at. Debbi had selected the number 28. You subtract that from 40, giving you 12.

So you just found out that the "good luck" number is 7. You count, "8, 9, 10, 11, 12." Once more you are stumped. "How old do you have to be before you're considered an adult?" If this doesn't get the right answer, you might try, "How much does a blackjack count?" or—if you're really desperate—, "How many shots in a twenty-one gun salute?" You're told 21. Repeat the number, and count, "22, 23, 24, 25, 26, 27, 28."

Ask Debbi the name of her card. Turn over the last one dealt. "There you are—twenty-eighth from the top!"

Here's the sequence:
Count 3: What's the unlucky number?
Count 3: How many lives does a cat have?
Count 3: What's the lucky number?
Subtract the selected number from 40, giving you the next

number you stop at. Ask, "How old do you have to be before you're considered an adult?"

◆ The Comeback Card ◆

A flourish or two can enhance a performance, and this one is quite easy to learn. You toss a card out, and it returns to you.

With your right hand, take off the top card of the deck and hold it at the outer end with the thumb on top, the first finger resting on the left outer edge, and the other fingers curled beneath (Illus. 50). Turn your hand counterclockwise as far as possible.

Spin the card out at about a 45° angle, snapping your hand back as the card is about to leave your hand. The card should go out several feet and then spin back towards your hand. With a little practice you should be able to catch it between thumb on top and fingers beneath.

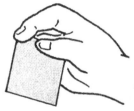

Illus. 50. With your right hand, take off the top card of the deck and hold it at the outer end with the thumb on top, the first finger resting on the left outer edge, and the other fingers curled beneath.

Illus. 51. The card is lightly held at the upper right corner between the right first and second fingers.

◆ Tossing Cards ◆

If, for some reason, you'd like to sail card after card to the far end of the room, the knack can be easily acquired.

The card is lightly held at the upper right corner between the right first and second fingers (Illus. 51). As with *The Comeback Card* (page 115), you bend your hand back counterclockwise. Aiming slightly upwards, spin the card outwards. Don't snap your wrist back, however. In fact, follow through a bit with the right hand.

In *The Comeback Card*, the card is snapped out quite violently; this move must be smooth and flowing. If your card keeps fluttering to the floor, it's probably because you're rushing.

◆ Cutback ◆

Holding the deck in your left hand, extend it slightly towards a spectator, asking if he'd like to cut the cards. But before he can even reach, you've quickly cut them with an absurdly easy flourish. "It's all right. I've taken care of it."

Hold the cards high in your left hand. Your thumb is on the left side, your first finger is at the front, and your other fingers are on the right side (Illus. 52). The tip of your first finger extends about halfway up the deck. Your left hand is about 9″ in front of your body. Your right hand is held below your chest, a few inches below the level of the deck; your hand is held cupped, waiting to catch the bottom portion of the deck (Illus. 53).

Illus. 52. Hold the cards high in your left hand. Your thumb is on the left side, your first finger is at the front, and your other fingers are on the right side.

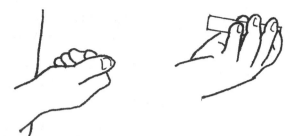

Illus. 53. Your left hand is about 9" in front of your body. Your right hand is held below your chest, a few inches below the level of the deck; your hand is held cupped, waiting to catch the bottom portion of the deck.

With a quick movement of your left first finger, snap the bottom portion of the deck back. The cards should hit an inch or so above your right hand and drop into that hand. Bring these cards forward with the right hand and complete the cut by dropping them on top of the deck.

CHALLENGES

"I can do it, but you can't!" An occasional challenge provides variety and balance to a program of card tricks. The following are clever and entertaining.

♦ Aces High ♦

At a poker game, or when conversation swings to gambling, you might point out a simple truth: "You can't beat four aces with a royal flush."

Someone is bound to object. If you have a deck of cards, take out the four aces. "Okay, now take out a royal flush."

Eventually, everyone will figure out that you cannot make a royal flush without an ace. And *you* have all the aces.

If you don't have a deck of cards, explain it like this: "Let's assume that I've taken the four aces from the deck. Which cards will you have in your royal flush?"

◆   A Good Flick   ◆

"Ladies and gentlemen," you begin. "I am once more going to attempt the impossible. I am going to perform a feat of magic with both a coin and a playing card. Thank you."

Balance a playing card on the first finger of your left hand. Balance a quarter on the card (Illus. 54). You must first balance the card on your finger and then the quarter; if you put the quarter on the card and balance the two together, this little trick might not work.

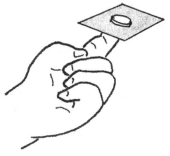

Illus. 54. Balance a playing card on the first finger of your left hand. Balance a quarter on the card.

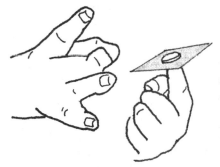

Illus. 55. Sharply flick the card from beneath the quarter by pressing the second finger of your right hand against your thumb, and then snapping it firmly against the card.

"I am going to magically remove the card and leave the quarter balanced on my finger." When the waves of skepticism have receded, sharply flick the card from beneath the quarter by pressing the second finger of your right hand against your thumb (Illus. 55), and then snapping it firmly against the card. You will probably require a few minutes of practice before you get the knack. The first time it worked for me, I was astonished to see the quarter still perched on my finger.

♦ No Heart ♦

Make this proposition to a volunteer: "Shuffle the deck. Give me half the cards and you keep half. We'll simultaneously deal off cards one at a time from our pile. I'll bet that you turn up a heart before I do."

The piles are left on the table. Each of you deals off the top card and turns it face up. As you take yours, however, draw it off towards you so that you can see its face before dealing it out. Deal other suits face up; when you come to a heart, deal it face down on your pile. Continue dealing along with the spectator, placing any hearts face down, until finally he objects.

Chances are, however, when he sees you deal that first card face down, he will turn it over, declaring himself the winner. You will be delighted to point out that you didn't turn the heart over, *he* did.

Before you have to resort to skullduggery, you might well win a few times, in which case you can restate the challenge and continue on.

♦ In Your Hat ♦

Besides a deck of cards, you'll need a hat, a wastebasket, a small cardboard box, or a large paper bag.

Challenge: "We each take ten cards and drop them one at a time, trying to put them into the hat on the floor. We must stand straight and drop the cards from no lower than waist level."

You demonstrate by dropping a card, holding it at one end. This is what is known as *misdirection* (or—if you prefer—*cheating*), for very few cards held in this manner will drop into the hat.

All who wish one get a turn. When you do it, however, hold each card flat before you release it. Be sure to release both ends simultaneously. Your card will tend to float down into the receptacle in a relatively straight line.

MISCELLANEOUS

You'll find some of the most astonishing card tricks ever invented in this section.

♦ I've Got Your Number ♦

Look through the deck and take out a spot card—a four, for example. Place it face down on the table, letting no one else see its face. Ask a volunteer to also remove a spot card (from 2 to 9), without letting you see it. Point to the right of your card and ask the spectator to place his card face down there.

Direct your helper to do the following: Double the value of his card, add two, multiply by five, and subtract six.

Assume his card was an eight. He doubles it, getting 16; adds two, making 18; times five makes 90; minus six makes 84.

You ask for the total. He says 84. You say, "Eighty-four . . . eight, four." Turn over the card on your right—eight; turn over the other—four.

The secret is in the last number, the one that the spectator subtracts. To arrive at this number, subtract from ten the value of the card you placed on the table. In our example, you placed down a four. Subtract from ten, and you get six—the number you have him subtract.

You may repeat the trick, using a different value spot card.

◆   The More Things Change   ◆

Give the cards to a spectator. Turn away and give these directions, with appropriate pauses: "Give the cards a shuffle. Cut the deck into two piles. Please think of a number from one to ten. Pick up one of the piles and look at the card at that number. Set the pile down. Pick up the other pile and deal that same number on top of the pile containing your card."

Pause. "Obviously, there is no way I could know where your card is. Please hand me the pile containing your card."

With your back still to the spectators, take the pile and bring it in front of you. Count the cards from hand to hand, pushing every other card up, starting with the first card. When you reach twenty cards, close up the cards sideways. Strip out the cards protruding from the top and place them on the bottom of the pile. Bring the cards forward.

"What number did you think of?" Count off that number face down. "And what was your chosen card?" Turn over the last card dealt off. The chosen card is back at its original number.

◆   Restored Deck   ◆

When you get a chance, sneakily turn over the bottom card so that it is the only face-up card in the deck. Spread the cards from hand to hand, showing that all the cards face the same way. Make sure you do not reveal the bottom face-up card.

Cut off half the deck with your right hand and rapidly move your hands apart. As you do so, turn your left hand over so that it's palm down. The larger movement completely conceals the turnover. Place the cards in your right hand beneath those in your left so that half of a face-up card shows. Apparently, you have two halves of the deck facing each other.

Regrip the cards in your left hand. Turn your left hand over so that it's palm down, showing the other side of the cards.

Note that your left hand conceals the face-up card. Immediately turn your left hand back.

Push the two halves of the deck together. Turn the deck over three times end for end. With your right hand, take off the top and bottom cards. Tap the deck with these, and set them aside. Spread the cards from hand to hand, showing that all the cards now face the same way.

You may do a repeat by reversing two cards at the bottom before beginning. When you fan through the cards to show that once again they all face the same way, make sure you stop a few cards before the bottom, reversed, card. Close the cards up and repeat the stunt.

◆   The Spectator's Trick   ◆

Suppose Donna insists that you perform another card trick. Say, "Why don't *you* perform one for me?"

Hand her the deck and tell her to shuffle it. Then she is to turn the cards' faces towards you and fan through, one card at a time, for you to make a selection. You note the *suit* of the top card and the *value* of the second card from the top. Let's assume that the top card is the seven of spades and that the second card is the four of hearts. You will be watching for the four of spades. If the spectator doesn't fan too neatly, feel free to separate some of the cards yourself. When she fans to that card, remove it from the deck, letting no one else see it. Place it face down to one side.

"Your job is to figure out what my card is. Close up the deck and turn it face down. Now if I were doing the trick, I'd deal the cards into a face-down pile until I got tired. That's always a good technique. Why don't you try that?"

When she finishes dealing, ask her to shuffle the rest of the cards and set them aside. The shuffle is strictly a diversionary tactic. She now picks up the pile she dealt off and, alternating the placement of the cards, deals it into two piles. "Turn over one of the top cards," you direct.

Suppose she turns over the seven of spades. "Good! You got the suit—spades. Turn over the other top card." She turns over the four of hearts. "A four! You got the value. Four of spades." Turn over the card you selected. Obviously, if she turns over the value card first, you reverse the procedure.

Be sure to congratulate your helper on her superb magical ability.

When the spectator begins to fan the cards before you, it's possible that the first two cards will be of the same suit or value. If so, point out that the cards don't look sufficiently mixed; another shuffle is required.

♦   The Disappearing Card   ♦

The effect was invented by Nick Trost and modified by Stewart Judah. This is my variation.

Have a card selected in the usual manner. Let the spectator hang on to the card for a moment. Perform the "Braue Turnover," as explained in *The Braue Force*, page 36. As you bring up the first face-up packet, say, "You could have chosen this card . . . " As you bring up the second, say, " . . . or this one . . . " Fan through the deck, showing about three-quarters of the cards. Note and remember the second card from the face of the deck. Say, " . . . or any of these. Instead, you chose . . . " Take the card from him, turn it face up, and name it. Place the card on the back of the deck. Turn the deck over.

You now have the face-down chosen card on top with a face-up card below it. All the other cards are face down, and you know the name of the second card from the bottom. Cut off about half the cards and complete the cut. Then cut off about a quarter of the deck and complete the cut. This brings the chosen card about 13 to 18 cards from the top.

Tap the deck. "I believe I've made your card disappear. Let's check." Deal cards from the top face up into a pile. Watch for the card you noted as second from the bottom. After you deal this card face up, deal one more card. Be very careful not to push off an extra card and reveal the face-up card beneath.

"No luck. Let's check the bottom cards." Turn the deck face up and deal off about fifteen cards onto the same group on the table.

"Still no good. Let's try the other side again." Turn the deck face down. Cut off all but about seven cards and turn them face up on top of the deck, making sure they're squared up. Deal off the face-up cards one at a time onto the pile until you come to a face-down card. Again, be very careful, because the card below this—the chosen card—is face up.

"It has to be among the rest." Turn the packet face up. Take off the first card, turn it face down, and place it at the back of the group. Continue until you come to the face-down card. Once more, you must be cautious.

Turn the packet face up and drop it on top of the cards on the table. Collect the face-up cards, even them up, and turn the deck face down. Cut the cards around the middle. Riffle the cards at the ends and then spread them out on the table. Face up in the middle is the chosen card.

♦ The Flying Cards ♦

You have three cards in your pocket. Ask a volunteer to cut a packet off the deck and place it in his pocket. "Now please count the rest of the cards."

Suppose the spectator counts 34 cards. Pick them up and place them in your pocket with the other three.

"So I have 34 cards," you say. "And you have 18."

Snap your fingers three times, waving your hand from the spectator's pocket to yours. "I'm trying to transfer three cards from your packet to mine. Please take out your cards and check the count."

He counts his pile. There are 15; three are missing. Remove your pile from your pocket (including the three extra cards) and have the spectator count them. The number is now 37.

MASTERY LEVELS CHART & INDEX

False Hindu Shuffle	9			★
Flying Cards	124	★		
Follow the Leader	74	★		
Gentle Persuasion	52		★	
Glide	10		★	
Good Flick	118		★	
Good Indication	64	★		
Great Expectorations	102	★		
Hair Pull	109		★	
Hindu Shuffle	7		★	
Hindu Shuffle Force	33			★
Houdini Knows	62	★		
I Love the Piano	44	★		
Impossible Prediction	21	★		
In My Pocket	103	★		
Invisible Deck—1	106		★	
Invisible Deck—2	108	★		
In Your Hat	119	★		
It *Is* Magic	15	★		
I've Got Your Number	120	★		
Jacks Be Nimble	49			★
Joiners	47	★		
Known Leaper	42		★	
Let Me Spell It Out	108		★	
Lucky Seven	61	★		
Magic Spell	16		★	
Matter of Choice	78	★		
Middle Key	71	★		
"Milking" Trick	65	★		
Miraskill Simplified	84	★		
Mixed Colors	88	★		
More Things Change	121	★		
Mystic Nine	13	★		
My Time Is Your Time	14	★		

Upsy-Daisy	69			★
Wandering Ace	98		★	
What's in a Name?	69	★		
What's the Difference?	51	★		
What's the Name of that Card?	67		★	
World Revisited	89	★		